APR 2 4 2010

PELLISSIPPI STATE
LIBRARY SERVICES
P. O. BOX 22990
KNOXVILLE, TN 37933-0990

THOUGHT MANIPULATION

THOUGHT MANIPULATION

The Use and Abuse of Psychological Trickery

Sapir Handelman

PRAEGER
An Imprint of ABC-CLIO, LLC

A B C C L I O

Santa Barbara, California • Denver, Colorado • Oxford, England

Copyright © 2009 by Sapir Handelman

All rights reserved. No part of this publication may be reproduced, stored in a retrieval system, or transmitted, in any form or by any means, electronic, mechanical, photocopying, recording, or otherwise, except for the inclusion of brief quotations in a review, without prior permission in writing from the publisher.

Library of Congress Cataloging-in-Publication Data

Thought manipulation : the use and abuse of psychological trickery / Sapir Handelman.
    p. cm. —
  Includes bibliographical references and index.
  ISBN 978–0–313–35532–5 (hard copy : alk. paper) — ISBN 978-0-313-35533-2 (ebook : alk. paper)
1. Control (Psychology). 2. Mental suggestion. 3. Behavior modification. I. Title.
BF611.H35 2009
153.8′5—dc22   2009009899

13 12 11 10 9   1 2 3 4 5

This book is also available on the World Wide Web as an eBook.
Visit www.abc-clio.com for details.

ABC-CLIO, LLC
130 Cremona Drive, P.O. Box 1911
Santa Barbara, California 93116-1911

This book is printed on acid-free paper ∞

Manufactured in the United States of America

In memory of my parents, Miriam and Joseph, and for my beloved wife, Yael.

Contents

Introduction		ix
1	The Manipulation Phenomenon: An Overview	1
2	The Topography of Manipulation	21
3	Freedom of Choice and the Ethics of Manipulation	31
4	Four Types of Manipulation	45
5	Introducing Manipulations That Limit Us	49
6	Spotlight on Advertising: The Free Market and Manipulation	51
7	Spotlight on Politics: Intellectual Manipulation	83
8	Spotlight on Leadership: Manipulative Peacemakers	99
9	Introducing Manipulations That Open Our Minds	111
10	Spotlight on Therapy: Therapeutic Manipulation	119
11	Liberation by Manipulation	141
12	Conclusion	153
Bibliography		155
Index		161

Introduction

THE CHALLENGE OF MANIPULATION

Manipulation is a wide-ranging phenomenon, present in almost every dimension of our social life. It is a puzzling motivating action geared towards interference in the decision-making process of another person, usually without his approval. This kind of intrusion is done indirectly by employing morally questionable tricks, such as temptation, distraction, and misdirection.

The trickery quality associated with manipulation enables the phenomenon to appear in almost infinite variations and under many different guises, from a powerful weapon in the service of indecent propaganda[1] to altruistic measures in psychotherapy and even education.[2] Indeed, social scientists have pointed out that an effective change in human decision-making and behavior cannot be achieved without employing a certain degree of manipulation.[3]

Manipulation is not exactly persuasion, not precisely coercion, and not merely similar to deception. This elusive phenomenon is located somewhere in the gray area between those motivating actions, and this gray place presents essential difficulties in characterizing manipulation and measuring its impact.

The skilled manipulator adopts strategies in a way that will obscure normative and legal judgment of his actions. His sophisticated and illusive methods of influence challenge the wisdom of leading proponents of the open society. The challenge appears in almost any dimension one can imagine, from politics to advertising to education and even to the most intimate relationships. For example, where is the limit between sexual harassment and legitimate courtship? How can decent and indecent propaganda be distinguished? Where exactly is the boundary between fair and unfair influence upon consumers? How can people's attention be attracted to innovative ideas when they aren't inclined to pay attention? How can the social reformer, the genius, and the pioneer challenge the conventional wisdom and open new vistas? What is the most effective way to open a public debate on sensitive, important issues that almost everyone in society regards as taboo?

This book proposes that the phenomenon of manipulation be used as a constructive tool. It introduces manipulative strategies in order to present difficulties that relate to one basic and fundamental question: How can an individual's autonomy, independence, and freedom of choice be guaranteed and decision-making be improved according to his or her preferences, priorities, and best interests?

LIMITING THE DISCUSSION TO THE "TWILIGHT ZONE"

The kinds of manipulation discussed in this book are geared toward influencing the decision-making of a person, but without physically limiting his options. Thus, the type of manipulation studied in this book will pertain to mental influence as opposed to physical coercion.[4] This distinction points to a fundamental difficulty in any discussion on the ethical and political aspects of manipulation: How can we protect the individual from destructive manipulation that cannot be quantified or clearly identified? Is the target of manipulation, who seems to act against his own best interests, acting out of a free choice, or is the adroit manipulator controlling him by preying on his weaknesses? Where is the boundary between irresistible weaknesses and free choice?

Our inability to read minds and thoughts obstructs us from finding satisfactory answers to just such tricky questions. Therefore, instead of tackling these problems head on, we shall turn to the bigger picture, which is the debate over the decent social order. The basic idea is that a stable, decent society can benefit its members while reducing the impact of damaging influences, such as offensive manipulation. However, is such a vision practically possible and, if so, how?

Introduction

THE STRUCTURE OF THE BOOK

The chief purpose of this book is to present challenging and arousing questions regarding individual freedom of choice via the analysis of manipulative strategies. The manipulations are analyzed through the eyes of a rational motivator, and questions, problems, and dilemmas are then constructed from possible outcomes of the actual dynamic interactions likely to create unexpected results.

The book is composed of three parts. The first part, which consists of the first four chapters, presents the concept of manipulation and explains the challenges the phenomenon presents to proponents of the open society. The second part, chapters 5 through 8, specifically introduces manipulations that are designed to limit our freedom of choice. The third part, chapters 9 through 11, discusses manipulations that are geared toward helping us discover new options, possibilities, and horizons.

Part One offers a general introduction to the phenomenon of manipulation and the problems it encompasses. It discusses the characteristics of manipulation, the ethics of manipulation, and the terminology of manipulation. The intention is to prepare the groundwork for the book as a whole.

Our point of departure is a rational human being who is determined to manipulate. This point of view helps to better understand the fundamental nature of manipulation and its uniqueness in comparison to other motivating actions, such as coercion, persuasion, and deception. However, social life does not provide laboratory conditions in human design. The next parts, which include many practical examples, examine actual manipulative interaction in the field.

The focus of Part Two, "limiting manipulations," aims to narrow the target's perception of available options. Usually the intention is to steer him toward one specific goal, without using coercive means. This part explores the problem of limiting manipulations in three dimensions: advertising, politics, and leadership.

The chapter on advertising focuses on "irrational" methods of influence employed by professional advertisers and the challenges raised thereby to proponents of capitalism, a society conducted and organized as a free market system.[5] The discussion of manipulative strategies and their effectiveness clarifies central issues at the very core of the capitalist view, such as the use of knowledge in society, the problem of censorship in advertisements, and the meaning of competition in the global social context. The upshot of this chapter is a demonstration of how an ideal free market is able to spontaneously reduce the impact of damaging influences. Still, the question remains: how is such an ideal approached?

The chapter on politics compares two manipulative strategies that appeared in two different election campaigns. This comparison—which emphasizes major differences with regard to parameters such as influence on voters, potential to shift voting, and legislation implications—indicates that rules intended to ensure fair elections can yield embarrassing, and even absurd, results. The inevitable conclusion is that even the most sophisticated, best-intended rules are only man-made and, thus, can fail. How can we improve the rules intended to direct a straight, effective, and beneficial political process?

The chapter on leadership focuses on a desperate situation of destructive social conflict. It presents a drastic political move that led to a turning point in one of the most entrenched conflicts in the world: the Arab-Israeli conflict. The chapter intends to demonstrate a basic rule in the art of political influence: not all forms of subversive manipulation are wrong. How can tolerable and intolerable manipulation be distinguished? How can manipulation be judged as ethical or unethical? What are the ethical limits of political manipulation?

Manipulations that are designed to expand people's perception are the topic of Part Three of this book. "Expanding manipulations" aim to open the target's mind to discover new horizons without directly intervening in his final decision. They are built to give a liberal response to painful situations of rigidity and inflexibility.

The manipulator, who wants to reveal other options to a target, believes that the target is possessed by a biased conviction that he refuses to examine critically. The manipulator in this case tries to cast doubts in the target's mind about the value of the target's conviction. In this way, the manipulator hopes to aid the target in improving his decision-making process. However, many bothersome questions and problems emerge from this scenario. Is this kind of liberation, liberation by manipulation, really possible? Is it possible to ensure that the liberal manipulator does not become an oppressive manipulator who actually maneuvers the target to agree to his opinion? Is it always advantageous to cast doubts on someone's convictions if he might not have other tools to cope with reality?

To better understand these issues, I examine psychological therapy as a laboratory for the study of central issues concerning the individual's freedom of choice, autonomy, and independence. The discussion connects the laboratory conditions of the psychological treatment and the ethical-political discussion in the field. The laboratory conditions of psychotherapy can help explore many difficulties in understanding manipulative interactions. For example, it helps demonstrate that it is not always clear who is actually directing the manipulative interface. A skilled manipulator might possibly be a victim of his own manipulation.

In conclusion, this book offers a preliminary study on a fascinating, pervading social phenomenon. By examining manipulation, it is possible to illuminate gray areas of human relations. This book will, hopefully, pave the way for further ethical and political discussions concerning how to develop the foundations of a good society.

NOTES

1. Adorno, T. W. (1951), "Freudian Theory and the Pattern of Fascist Propaganda" in *The Essential Frankfurt School Reader*. Ed. Andrew Arato and Eike Gebhardt. (New York: Urizen, 1978), 118–137.

2. A manipulative approach to cope with human problems and misery can be found in Watzlawick, P., J. H. Weakland, and R. Fisch, (1974), *Change: Principles of Problem Formation and Problem Resolution* (New York and London: W. W. Norton & Company). The authors, who are professional therapists, offer manipulative strategies to deal with stubborn psychological problems.

3. Kelman, H. C. (1965), "Manipulation of Human Behavior: An Ethical Dilemma for the Social Scientist," *Journal of Social Issues* 21, no. 2: 33. Kelman, who agrees that an "effective behavior change inevitably involves some degree of manipulation," presents and analyzes a dilemma for the social scientist: "The two horns of the dilemma, then, are represented by the view that any manipulation of human behavior inherently violates a fundamental value, but that there exists no formula for so structuring an effective change situation that such manipulation is totally absent."

4. The classical distinction between liberty (physical options available for a person) and autonomy (the individual's ability to choose among the available options) indicates that, principally, manipulation invades the autonomy of an individual without limiting his or her liberty. In other words, manipulation influences mainly the mental sphere (autonomy) and not the physical one (liberty). For a further discussion on the distinction between liberty and autonomy, see Dworkin, G. (1997), *The Theory and Practice of Autonomy* (New York: Cambridge University Press), 14.

5. I focus mainly on Friedman, R. & M. (1979), *Free to Choose: A Personal Statement* (New York and London: Harcourt Brace Jovanovich); Hayek, F. A.

(1944), *The Road to Serfdom* (Chicago: University of Chicago Press); Hayek, F. A. (1945), "The Use of Knowledge in Society," *American Economic Review* xxxv, No. 4: 519–530; Hayek, F. A. (1960), *The Constitution of Liberty* (Chicago: University of Chicago Press); Hayek, F. A. [1973] (1993a), *Rules and Order*, Volume 1 of *Law, Legislation and Liberty* (London: Routledge and Kegan Paul); Hayek, F. A. [1979] (1993b), *The Political Order of a Free People*, Volume 3 of *Law, Legislation and Liberty* (London: Routledge and Kegan Paul).

CHAPTER 1
The Manipulation Phenomenon: An Overview

INTRODUCTION

Manipulation is an interesting motivating action. It is not exactly coercion, not precisely persuasion, and not entirely similar to deception. It is a widespread phenomenon that occurs in almost all walks of life: politics, art, education, and even interpersonal relations. Yet, the professional literature that attempts to cope with the challenge of systematically characterizing and analyzing the very essence of the phenomenon remains insufficient.

Very little academic work has been done to explore, investigate, and explain the fundamental nature of manipulation and its uniqueness relative to other motivating actions. Most of the work that attempts to face this challenge assembles and summarizes the phenomenon into one conclusive definition. I would like to open my own discussion of manipulation by presenting three definitions that have helped me greatly in understanding the important aspects of manipulation, especially in exploring the uniqueness of the phenomenon and the secrets behind its powerful influence.

Joel Rudinow, in a discussion about the unique characteristics of manipulation, observes that "most people...would distinguish manipulation from persuasion, on one hand, and from coercion, on the other."[1] He emphasizes the sophistication of the phenomenon and proposes the following complicated definition: "A attempts to manipulate S if A attempts the complex motivation of S's behavior by means of deception or by playing on a supposed weakness of S."[2] Robert Goodin, who is interested in the ethical aspects of manipulatory politics, regards manipulative behavior as an exercise of power.[3] He emphasizes the trickery-based features of manipulation and proposes a friendlier definition than Rodinow's: "One person manipulates another when he deceptively influences him, causing the other to act contrary to his putative will."[4] Michael J. Philips, who explores the ethical aspects of manipulation in advertising, emphasizes the irrational motifs inherent in the phenomenon. He clearly understands that manipulation is neither persuasion nor deception and proposes the following sophisticated definition to manipulative advertising: "... we might first describe it as advertising involving efforts to nonpersuasively alter consumers' perceptions of products by means other than deception."[5]

Each of these thinkers emphasizes different important aspects and elements of manipulation, including sophistication (Rudinow), trickery (Goodin), and irrational motifs (Phillips). These differences help to concretize the impossibility of assembling and summarizing the very essence of manipulation in one clear and conclusive definition. There will always be important examples of manipulations (or, more precisely, what we intuitively categorize as manipulative behavior) that contradict each definition or, at least, are not included under the umbrella of that definition.[6]

In this book, which focuses on manipulation in a very broad sense, I intend to use a different methodology. Like Rudinow, Goodin, and Phillips, I will propose my own definition of manipulation. Unlike these thinkers, however, my proposal is much more humble and not as ambitious. I will offer a broad and general definition only as a point of departure and as an introduction to my main analysis. The main focus will turn to a sketch of the landscape of manipulation through a systematic analysis of the unique characteristics of the phenomenon and the necessary conditions for it to occur (an overview that definition alone cannot provide).[7]

I will begin by asking the questions: What does a rational human being, who wishes to be manipulative, have to do? Which effect does he desire to create? What motivates him to employ manipulative tricks? Taking up these questions is intended to facilitate our preliminary discussion. Exploring the issue from this point of view is helpful in forming a better understanding of the unique characteristics of manipulation and allows us to avoid struggling with trickery questions that cannot be satisfactorily answered. (For example, how could we identify manipulative interaction?) I will simply try to examine a manipulative interface as it is designed in the laboratory of a rational manipulator.

Of course, to remain exclusively in the laboratory of a rational manipulator seems to evade the very challenge of coming to grips with manipulative behavior. The reason is that almost every rational plan of manipulative strategy sooner or later must contend with dynamic interaction that is likely to yield unexpected results. The next chapters, which include many real-life examples, are conducted on the theoretical-practical axis. I begin with a rational motivator planning his moves; different possible outcomes of his strategy are the very stuff of actual political problems, ethical dilemmas, and intellectual challenges.

In conclusion, this introductory chapter is designed to sketch the landscape of our discussion, provoke critical thinking, and prepare the ground for understanding the challenges that the manipulation phenomenon presents to passionate advocates of liberty, autonomy, and the open society.

BASIC ASSUMPTIONS

This chapter intends to feature the unique characteristics of manipulation in an analytical form and present typical characteristics of a manipulative interaction.[8] For this purpose, I found it useful and efficient to employ certain basic assumptions that are usable in economic analysis. This kind of move is consistent with the methodology known as Economic Imperialism.[9]

Our basic assumptions, which are based on simple common sense, are intended to facilitate our discussion. As our journey progresses, I will need to deviate from basic assumptions and even cast doubts upon their validity. The following chapters include many practical examples. As sophisticated and logical as our assumptions may sound, reality has its own rules of conduct. Real-life situations are not necessarily conducted according to our basic assumptions, to say the very least. This is especially true of manipulative interactions that contain elements that we tend to understand as irrational.

This book describes manipulative situations as a type of interaction that occurs between human beings. The analysis focuses on agents that hold "standard" human characteristics: conscience, preferences, will, and so on. The discussion is limited to conscious behavior (as much as possible).

As already stated, the book explores the unique characteristics of manipulation and presents the ethical challenges that the phenomenon raises. For this purpose, I wish to examine what leads a person to be manipulative, the method by which he chooses his actions, and the secrets behind the possible impacts of manipulative behavior. Accordingly, I will use standard rational assumptions to investigate the motivations of each agent. I will assume that every participant in the interaction is an autonomic agent that wishes to improve his conditions (to maximize his preferences) while, at the same time, he shies away from activity that might worsen his situation (to minimize his risk). One of the practical implications of this assumption is that every agent is risk averse and will prefer to stay in a current situation rather than make a change that might weaken his position.

It is important to emphasize that any political-ethical discussion on manipulative behavior, at least from a liberal perspective, presupposes that the environment offers the individual various options and does not restrict his activities to one definite possibility.

MANIPULATION AS A MOTIVATING ACTION

Manipulation is a motivating action. It is an attempt by one person to maneuver his fellow to act in a certain manner and/or for a specific goal. The choice to manipulate (maneuvering) and not employ a more direct approach indicates that the participants in the interaction hold contrasting positions. Robert Goodin, in his book *Manipulatory Politics*, presents and criticizes a neo-Marxist view that indicates the contradiction results from different interests: " ... manipulation necessarily works against the interests of those being manipulated."[10] From this point of view it is implicit that any motivating action that is employed for the benefit of the target could never be considered manipulation. In other words, the neo-Marxist claim omits an entire area of positive and half-positive manipulations that are directed to advance the target's interests. Goodin, who tries to propose an improved approach to the study of manipulative behavior, claims that the contradiction is driven by different wills and not necessarily by opposing interests; that it is "one person ... causing the other to act contrary to his putative will."[11]

Goodin's definition, which focuses on contradictory wills, presupposes that the target's will, or at least his putative will, is always clear to the manipulator. Often enough, however, human beings tend to speak in different and contradictory voices simultaneously, which makes it almost impossible to understand what they really want. Does it mean that they cannot be manipulated?

Take, for example, the wealthy housewife who constantly complains that the maintenance housework (cleaning, cooking, and shopping) causes her unhappiness, misery, and frustration, but, on the other hand, she persistently refuses to hire any help. How could we forget the miserable Don Juan, who wishes to get married, but, systematically, has love affairs only with married women? And, of course, there is the tragic case of the wonderful musician who devoted most of her life to studying the art of opera, but constantly avoids precious opportunities to audition in front of famous conductors who might be able to help her develop a professional career.

Our three tragic heroes—the frustrated house wife, the miserable Don Juan, and the desperate musician—provide concrete example that, many times, ambiguity regarding a person's will results from the fact that he himself is confused and cannot make up his mind. Ironically, even paradoxically, manipulative interference might be useful in helping the struggler realize his will and reach a decision. Indeed, many techniques in education and psychotherapy are designed to help a confused individual discover his will and decide what to do with it.[12]

Goodin's definition also seems problematic in situations where the manipulator and the target seem to share the same objectives. In those interactions, the motivation to employ a manipulative strategy can be driven by different perspectives on opportunities to satisfy the will, such as in cases where the target is desperate to satisfy his will and achieve his goals.

Accordingly, I propose to expand Goodin's definition and to see manipulation "as an indirect motivating action that is employed out of fear that a more direct and explicit approach will face resistance."[13] However, even this preliminary broad definition requires much care. In certain cases the decision to manipulate is based purely on efficiency whereby the manipulator strives to avoid long, tiring explanations and save time and effort. An extreme example is the leader who forecasts a political crisis that requires a quick response. He assumes that explaining the situation to his colleagues is a waste of a precious time and chooses to manipulate them instead.[14]

MANIPULATION CREATES AN ILLUSION OF FREE CHOICE

Manipulation is geared toward influencing the target to operate in a direction that under normal circumstances he would probably resist.

Moreover, many manipulative strategies are designed to lead the target to act in a way that is not consistent with his intentions, motivations, and best interests.

This characteristic of manipulative behavior sounds somewhat paradoxical. On the one hand, leading someone to act against his preferences and priorities indicates that manipulation contains compelling elements. On the other hand, the term manipulation itself, which is associated with an elusive concept such as "maneuvering," indicates that the target does have some judgment and consideration while he operates. This tension can be resolved by adding to our description of manipulative interaction the element of "illusory free choice."

In general, the sophisticated manipulator strives to intrude, interfere, and influence the decision-making process of the target by giving him the impression that he (the target) chooses his actions freely and independently. To achieve this effect, the manipulator attempts to maneuver the target to perceive the "intentional action" (i.e., the manipulator's goal) as the best available option in the current situation. Following our basic assumptions, especially those of maximizing preferences and minimizing risk, the target is obligated to take the best available action according to his understanding of the situation. The practical meaning is that the target, who is subject to a hidden influence, believes that his choices are made freely and independently.

Hiding relevant information in order to create a desired decision exemplifies the idea of "illusory free choice" in a manipulative interaction. The target, who believes that he chooses the best available option freely and independently, is actually subject to invisible interference in his judgment and critical thinking.

Unfortunately, it is not difficult to imagine opposite situations where a person is convinced that he is on the right track, making the best decisions and not willing to consider other options. Ironically, and even paradoxically, helping him to discover the value of other possibilities requires the application of the unconventional methods of influence that certain manipulative strategies can offer.

In the most difficult cases, the individual is trapped in a biased conception of reality that he is not willing to examine critically. There are many classic examples: the ambitious young gentleman who is determined to become a great musician even though he lacks any sense of rhythm; the brave general who refuses to accept the fact that the enemy is going to attack; the diligent manufacturer who spends most of his money, time, and effort improving the quality of goods that are no longer in demand.

Cases of tragic entrenchment are costly in that they limit the world perception of the trapped individual, damage his adaptation to the continually changing circumstances of reality, and cause him and his surroundings much misery and suffering. The important point is that a sophisticated manipulative strategy can sometimes be the only hope in such circumstances. An indirect method of influence can persuade the entrenched target to doubt the validity of his biased position. In this way the manipulator could help the entrenched target consider other options that he previously was not even prepared to acknowledge. Ironically, in the initial position the target was convinced that he was choosing the best available option, while it is the manipulative intervention that enabled him to make a real choice.

I label this kind of strategy "liberation by manipulation," and I address it extensively in the coming chapters. Here, I will mention briefly that this strategy involves methods of influence in psychotherapy and education that are designed to create the impression that the target is doing most of the changing by himself. He is not supposed to notice that someone else (i.e., the therapist or the educator) is actually maneuvering the situation and invisibly helping him discover the road to change and improvement. In the following chapters we will need to explore several issues associated with this strategy: How could the benevolent manipulator achieve this effect? Is "liberation by manipulation" really an effective strategy? What are the risks?

MANIPULATION IS HIDDEN FROM THE TARGET

Motivating by employing manipulative strategy intends to minimize any possibility of the target objecting to the manipulator's moves. The manipulator strives to prevent the target from considering certain operational possibilities or, alternatively, the manipulator attempts to maneuver the target to consider possible actions that he (the target) refuses to examine. The manipulator attempts to achieve the motivating effect smoothly and elegantly. He wishes to create the impression that the target is choosing his actions freely and independently (i.e., illusionary free choice).

This effect could be achieved because, in the time of a manipulative interaction and in the context of its subject, the manipulator's spectrum of vision is larger than the target's. It seems that the manipulator simply knows more. One of the practical implications is that at the time of the interaction the manipulator can adapt the target's point of view (later I will show that he actually has to do it), something that the target (who holds a smaller spectrum of vision) cannot do.[15] The inevitable conclusion is that during a manipulative interaction the target cannot identify that he operates under a manipulative influence.[16]

A good example is the act of seduction for indecent purposes. The sophisticated seducer estimates possible reactions to her future moves and thinks like the target while she plans the scam. However, the target, whose mind is distracted by strong feelings of passion and love, does not even consider the possibility that he is being led astray. The target's ability to identify the manipulator's real intentions enables him to consider options other than the manipulator's goal. This is exactly what the manipulator wishes to prevent—otherwise, she would not choose to manipulate. The practical meaning is that the "scam" has been exposed and the target can decide whether he wishes to surrender or refuse to act according to the manipulator's guidelines. In other words, it is not a case of "illusory free choice" but a real free choice. Therefore, the manipulative act fails or does not exist.[17]

According to our characterization, statements like "you are manipulating me" are self-contradictions. It is not possible to be a victim of manipulation and, at the same time, to know about it. Moreover, it is possible that this confronting approach was employed in order to change roles in the interaction. One option is that by leveling the accusation, I am trying to find out your hidden intentions. In a case where you do not see it, we have changed roles. I have become the manipulator and you the target.

Another option is to regard the statement "you are manipulating me" as an indirect message: "This time I am surrendering to you dear, but you have to know that you owe me." In a case where the manipulator does not see it, he becomes exposed to the possibility of a future pressure without being aware of it. The manipulator's spectrum of vision is, actually, smaller than the target's, and the practical meaning is that the original manipulator fell in his own trap and became a victim of manipulation.

MANIPULATION AFFECTS CRITICAL CAPACITY

Critical capacity is an important mechanism that helps us select our actions according to our priorities and preferences. It supposes to function like a dedicated guard whose duty is to keep our decisions and behavior consistent with our self-interest and world view.

A motivating action designed to lead a person to act in contradiction to his preferences without noticing the distortion must disrupt, or at least bypass, the inspection process. Accordingly, manipulative behavior necessarily intends to affect the target's critical capacity. I present two types of strategies that intend to achieve this effect. The first is designed to cloud, blur, and limit the target's critical capacity while the second, surprisingly, is geared toward improving the target's performance.

The first type is quite obvious. The manipulator employs morally questionable means during the interaction to diminish any possible objection to his moves by the target. As the next two examples demonstrate, however, affecting critical capacity can be used for different and even opposing goals and motivations. It could be applied for the benefit of the manipulator and it could be used to improve the target's position.

The first example promotes Erich Fromm's description of manipulative techniques that is used by modern advertising to neutralize critical judgment and promote the selling of useless—or, at least, unnecessary—goods: "A vast sector of modern advertising...does not appeal to reason but to emotion; like any other kind of hypnoid suggestion, it tries to impress its objects emotionally and then make them submit intellectually...All these methods are essentially irrational; they have nothing to do with the qualities of the merchandise, and they smother and kill the critical capacities of the customer like an opiate or outright hypnosis. They give him a certain satisfaction by their daydream qualities just as the movies do, but at the same time they increase his feeling of smallness and powerlessness."[18]

The second example is taken from the field of psychotherapy. Milton Erickson's confusion technique is simply designed to confuse the target. The idea is to paralyze the target's critical capacity and maneuver him to operate in a direction contradictory to his intentions and priorities: "Particularly did I recall the occasion on which my physics laboratory mate had told his friends that he intended to do the second (and interesting) part of a coming experiment and that he was going to make me do the first (and onerous) part of the experiment. I learned of this, and when we collected our experimental material and apparatus and were dividing it up into two separate piles, I told him at the crucial moment quietly but with great intensity, 'That sparrow really flew to the right, then suddenly flew left, and then up, and I just don't know what happened after that.' While he stared blankly at me, I took the equipment for the second part of the experiment and set busily to work, and he, still bewildered, merely followed my example by setting to work with the equipment for the first part of the experiment. Not until the experiment was nearly completed did he break the customary silence that characterized our working together. He asked, 'How come I'm doing this part? I wanted to do that part.' To this I replied simply, 'It just seemed to work out naturally this way.' "[19]

In general, Erickson developed and used the confusion technique for hypnosis. Later, he and others employed the confusion technique in psychotherapy to confuse the patient as a preparation for a beneficial change. The confusion works to lower the patient's critical judgment and paralyze his usual resistance to changing old habits that cause him so much suffering. By lowering the target's critical awareness, Erickson hoped to open him up to discover new ways.[20]

The second strategy, surprisingly, is designed to develop, improve, and even enrich the target's critical capacity. However, we should not forget that affecting critical capacity is part of a manipulative strategy. In the final account, manipulation intends to lead the target to act in a manner that he would otherwise have rejected, objected to, and refused. We have good reason to suspect that the sophisticated manipulator only wishes to create the impression of helping the target to improve, develop, and elaborate his critical capacity. The real intention is quite the opposite.

The next example, which presents a manipulative workshop for developing critical capacity, demonstrates this issue. A matchmaker is hired to find the perfect bride for a young, ultra-orthodox Jew. The young gentleman, who devotes most of his time to biblical studies, has never dated a lady in his short lifetime. As an excellent student, he quickly learns from his new mentor (the matchmaker) that the value of the bride is measured according to the status of her family. "The key to successful marriage," repeats the matchmaker, "is that the bride comes from a good family." Equipped with this valuable knowledge, our young hero comes to his first date to meet an unattractive, spoiled lady whose rich father "accidently" paid the matchmaker a lot of money.

Ironically, funny stories about manipulative strategies in old-fashioned societies resemble serious methods of sales promotion in modern economies. Many times we need to buy a device whose functions we do not understand, and we do not know how to compare between different products. We enter the shop cautiously and insecurely and, immediately, an elegant salesman offers his assistance. Our new guide demonstrates an impressive professional knowledge—

of which we cannot appreciate its real value—and patiently explains how to pick the best product and what sort of performance we should expect from quality goods. However, our dedicated teacher, whose main job is sales and not education (a simple fact that we tend to forget) presents criteria that emphasizes the advantages of the goods he wishes to sell and distract attention from their disadvantages.

The more trivial cases are those where the manipulator has a good estimation of the target's flavors, preferences, and priorities. Nevertheless, the ability to affect critical capacity does not necessarily require such awareness. For example, it can be quite effective to use psychological knowledge and even mathematical expertise to maneuver a person's decision. A well-known technique is to formulate a decision-making problem in a way that would diminish any possible objection to the manipulator's desirable outcome: "An individual's choice can be reversed by framing a given choice problem differently. If it is presented as a choice between gains, one will typically choose the less risky option. However, if it is presented as a choice between losses, then one will opt for the riskier option."[21]

In general, the manipulator influences the target's decisions by leading him to believe that he (the target) chooses the best available alternative (according to his preferences and priorities) in a given situation. The target's understanding or, more precisely, misunderstanding of the circumstances indicates that his critical capacity is clouded, blurred, and even paralyzed. The manipulator is able to achieve this effect by various means: distraction, temptation, misdirection, rational arguments, and so on. This issue will be dealt with extensively in later chapters, where I present different types of manipulative strategies and include practical examples. For this general characterization of manipulation, the crucial point is that manipulative behavior, as desirable as it may be, aims to diminish the target's ability to judge critically the manipulator's moves.

THE MOTIVATING ELEMENT IN MANIPULATIVE INTERACTION

We have seen that an important characteristic of a manipulative interaction is the target's belief that the "intentional action" (i.e., the manipulator's goal) is the best available option for him in a given situation. Accordingly, the manipulator's ability to affect critical capacity in order to distort judgment may lower the target's awareness, but it does not necessarily guarantee a twist in the "right" direction.

To put it differently, blurring, clouding, and paralyzing critical capacity does not promise motivation toward the "desirable" track. A strong incentive is needed to guarantee that the intentional action takes priority in the target's scale of preferences. In order to achieve this effect, the manipulator strives to create a link between the intentional action and the fulfillment of a powerful wish.

Often enough the manipulator approaches, stimulates, or even creates a powerful wish or a strong desire in the target's mind. He gives the impression that fulfillment, or satisfaction, can be achieved if the target follows the manipulator's guidelines. Note, for example, the profitable and efficient strategy to promote the sale of soap, as described by Jeffrey Trachtenberg in an article that appeared in *Forbes* in 1987: "Women would pay 25 cents for a bar of soap that made their hands clean but $2.50 for a bar of soap that promised to make their hands beautiful. Selling plain soap was peddling product performance. But add some skin cream and you are selling hope—psychologically more powerful, economically more profitable."[22]

In contrast to this strategy, the link between the intentional action (the manipulator's goal) and the fulfillment of a wish can be formed into detachment. That is, the manipulator creates the impression that realizing the target's wish is impossible. In this way the manipulator tries to change the target's agenda. The following example, which presents an unusual way to escape from a desperate situation, illustrates this issue:

"When in 1334 the Duchess of Tyrol, Margareta Maultasch, encircled the castle of Hochosterwitz in the province of Carinthia, she knew only too well that the fortress, situated on an incredibly steep rock rising high above the valley floor, was impregnable to direct attack and would yield only to a long siege. In due course, the situation of the defenders became critical: they were down to their last ox and had only two bags of barley corn left. Margareta's situation was becoming equally pressing, albeit for different reasons: her troops were beginning to be unruly, there seemed to be no end to the siege in sight, and she had similarly urgent military business elsewhere. At this point the commandant of the castle decided on a desperate course of action which to his men must have seemed sheer folly: he had the last ox slaughtered, had its abdominal cavity filled with the remaining barely, and ordered the carcass thrown down the steep cliff onto a meadow in front of the enemy camp. Upon receiving this scornful message from above, the discouraged duchess abandoned the siege and moved on."[23]

The Manipulation Phenomenon: An Overview 13

The motivating wish as a stimulating instrument in a manipulative interaction shows another aspect of the gap in viewpoints between the manipulator and the target. The target is trying to fulfill a powerful wish or to satisfy a strong desire while the manipulator motivates him to do it by employing incentives that create a false impression.[24]

TWO TYPES OF MISLEADING

Manipulation is geared toward motivating the target to operate in a form that under normal conditions he would probably resist, object to, and reject. Manipulative interaction invites a meeting between opposing positions—the manipulator's and the target's positions. However, the meeting, or more precisely the clash, is mostly indirect, invisible, and covert. This effect is created by the trickery that is intrinsic to manipulative behavior. The use of morally questionable means, such as temptation, misdirection, and intimidation, contribute to the elusive feature of manipulation.

In order to better describe and concretize the sophistication of manipulation (at least relative to other motivating actions), I propose to distinguish between two types of misleading: simple misleading and complex misleading. The first type appears mostly in deception. The second type is employed mainly in motivating actions that can be better categorized as manipulation.[25]

In simple misleading interactions, the clash between the different positions is clear, direct, and frontal. For example: John points to Rome after Joseph has asked him to show him the road to Washington. To put it differently, John simply and clearly lies to Joseph. In this book, I am inclined to categorize this type of behavior as deception.

In complex misleading interactions, the clash between the different positions is indirect, invisible, and covert. Let us take, for example, an imaginary scenario that is not so far from reality. The heroine is an African-American lady who believes that America needs a drastic change. The African-American candidate for the presidency symbolizes for her a change in the desirable direction. She is not even willing to consider another option. However, the white candidate approaches her in a sophisticated manner. He appoints as his deputy a woman. This move reminds our African-American voter that besides her ethnic identity (African-American) she holds also a gender identity (woman). Since each side has the potential to make history (an African-American president or a female vice president) our African-American voter, who is a passionate advocate of civil rights, equity, and social justice, faces a dilemma. The meaning is that the white candidate sophisticatedly maneuvered her to consider voting for him, an idea that she hates to begin with.

In general, manipulative behavior includes direct and indirect communication. The direct messages are used to affect critical capacity and paralyze any objection to the manipulator's moves. The indirect messages intend to motivate the receiver to operate in a manner or for a cause that is controversial. Therefore, manipulation employs complex misleading tactics.

In our previous example, the direct message of the white candidate to the African-American voter is: "The time has come for America to have a female vice president," and the indirect message is: "Therefore, you need to vote for me, the white candidate." The clash between the different initial positions, the African-American voter's preference (an African-American president) and the white candidate's aspiration (to be a president), is indirect. Accordingly, we can classify the white candidate's political move as a manipulation.

MANIPULATION INTRUDES ON AUTONOMY WITHOUT LIMITING FREEDOM

The distinction between "freedom" and "autonomy" is extremely important to the characterization of the very essence of manipulative behavior, or at least to those motivating actions that I am labeling manipulation in this book. In general, freedom (or liberty) refers to the range of operational possibilities available to a person, while autonomy is related to his decision-making process concerning these options. The meaning is that freedom is related to the physical dimension while autonomy is connected to the mental sphere. Let me draw out this distinction by using John Lock's extreme example: "The person who ... is put into a cell and convinced that all the doors are locked (when, in fact, one is left unlocked) is free to leave the cell. But because he cannot—given his information—avail himself of this opportunity, his ability to do what he wishes is limited."[26] According to our distinction, the person has the freedom to leave, but he does not have the autonomy to do so because he believes that he is trapped.

In principle, the manipulator does not coerce, in the physical sense, the target to act, but uses cunning, sneaky, and tricky ways to influence, in the mental sense, his decision-making process. To put it differently, manipulative behavior is geared toward influencing the target's decisions, but without limiting his options. Accordingly, we can conclude that manipulation intrudes on the autonomy of the individual without limiting his freedom.

Of course, we should bear in mind that the possibility to object to, reject, and oppose any intrusion to our autonomic sphere is not always existent, even in theory. For example, hiding relevant information so that it is inaccessible can alter a decision-making process without any possibility of the decision-maker knowing about the distortion and raising protest. The crucial point is that these are exactly the cases that I would like to leave out of this discussion. The case where a motivator is able to invisibly control the external conditions and maneuver the target's decision-making without any possibility of the target knowing about and objecting to the alteration have an effect similar to coercion. Physical compulsion is not involved, but the distance from it is not too far. Accordingly, the contribution of these interactions to our discussion, the clarification of the unique characteristics of manipulation, and the challenges that the phenomenon presents to proponents of the open society is marginal.

The more interesting and challenging cases are those where it seems that the target can protest, oppose, and resist the manipulative influence, but he does not do so. Moreover, often enough it turns out that the target is actually cooperating with the manipulator even when it clearly contradicts his very best interests. This is a crucial point that will be discussed in detail, later. For now the main point is that the discussion is limited to cases where the target is able, or apparently able, to choose his actions freely and independently.

To better clarify what I will consider as manipulation in this book, let me distinguish between two ways of shaping external conditions, or in Kelman's term, "environmental manipulations"[27]: manipulations that are based upon the manipulator's ability to "construct the environment" and manipulations based upon the manipulator's attempt to "construct the target's vision upon the environment." In general, our discussion excludes the first type and includes the second. Constructing the environment means that the motivator has the ability to control the external conditions with little possibility of the target knowing about it and protesting. An example of this might be indecent trading, which intentionally moves prices for the purpose of misleading participants in the financial market.[28] Those cases seem to have an effect that is similar to coercion. Therefore, I will leave them out of our discussion.

In contrast, constructing the vision upon the environment means that the motivator presents a decision-making problem in a misleading, fallacious, and tendentious manner. These manipulations are quite common in voting and elections, when the agent who chairs the meeting has the power to determine the agenda. The manipulator uses sophisticated tools, such as mathematical and psychological knowledge, to structure the alternatives in a manner that maximizes the chances of a favorable outcome. The manipulator could be an expert in statistics, a professional psychologist, or a well-known specialist in social choice theories. Social interactions, however, usually do not occur in a vacuum. Therefore, it is not difficult to imagine that the layman target has good reasons to be suspicious, can ask for help, is able to consult with experts, and even to protest. Accordingly, at least to some extent, those manipulations belong to the landscape of our discussion.[29]

SUMMARY

This introductory chapter intends to give a general impression of the unique characteristics of the manipulation phenomenon. It seeks to cope with a very basic and fundamental question: What is a manipulative interaction?

I opened the discussion by proposing a broad, general, and non-binding definition: "Manipulation is an indirect motivating action that is employed out of fear that a direct approach might face a resistance." However, the idea is to use it only as a point of departure. This broad definition intends to stimulate critical thinking and provide a general orientation to the landscape of our discussion. The main analysis focused on exploring the necessary conditions for the phenomenon of manipulation to occur.

To facilitate the discussion, I proposed to examine the basic nature of manipulation from the standpoint of a rational human being who wishes to manipulate. What effects is the future manipulator hoping to create? What type of tactics does he intend to use? What are the possible outcomes of his moves? I have found eight major characteristics of manipulative interaction, as follows:

1. Manipulation is a motivating action.
2. Manipulation employs morally questionable means, such as temptation, misdirection, and intimidation.

3. Manipulation gives the target the illusion that he is able to choose his actions freely and independently.
4. Manipulation invisibly influences the target's decision-making process in that the target cannot identify that he operates under manipulative influence.
5. Manipulation affects the target's critical capacity.
6. Manipulation creates a link between the intentional action (the manipulator goal) and the fulfillment of an powerful wish or the satisfaction of a strong desire.
7. Manipulation employs complex misleading tactics whereby the clash between the positions of the manipulator and the target is designed to be indirect, invisible, and covert.
8. Manipulation intrudes on the target's autonomy (the mental dimension) without limiting his freedom (the physical sphere).

To make the exploration more interesting and challenging, I have restricted the discussion. Manipulative interactions in this book are social situations where the target seems to have the ability to resist, protest, and oppose the uninvited intervention in his decision-making process. To put it differently, despite the sophisticated intrusion, the impression is that the target still carries the ability to choose his actions freely and independently. Therefore, there is no escape from wondering, especially in manipulative interactions where the target acts clearly against his interests, aspirations, and even declarations: How much of a free choice does the target really have? Does the target only hold an illusion of free choice or is he actually able to choose his actions freely and independently? How does the manipulator achieve such a sophisticated motivating effect? Does manipulation involve magical work?

These are fundamental questions for any discussion of the ethical-political aspects and implications of manipulation. They are extremely important to any exploration in the spirit of the liberal tradition, which always defended the individual's liberty, independence, and freedom of choice. However, before we continue to examine the challenges that manipulation poses to proponents of the open society, we still need to get a better orientation of the topography of our discussion. Chapter 2 attempts to sketch manipulation relative to other motivating actions: coercion, persuasion, and deception.

NOTES

1. Rudinow (1978), "Manipulation," *Ethics* 88: 339.
2. Ibid. 346.
3. Goodin, R. E. (1980), *Manipulatory Politics* (New Haven and London: Yale University Press), 8.
4. Ibid., 19.
5. Phillips, M. J. (1997), *Ethics and Manipulation in Advertising: Answering a Flawed Indictment* (Westport, CT: Quorum), 17.
6. In this respect, Karl Popper has attacked the view that scientific inquiry depends upon the precision of terms: "In science, we take care that the statements we make should never depend upon the meaning of our terms ... This is why our terms make so little trouble. We do not overburden them. We try to attach to them as little weight as possible. We do not take their 'meaning' too seriously. We are always conscious that our terms are a little vague (since we have learned to use them only in practical applications) and we reach precision not by reducing their penumbra of vagueness, but rather by keeping well within it, by carefully phrasing our sentences in such a way that the possible shades of meaning of our terms do not matter." Popper, K. R. [1945] (1996), *The Open Society and Its Enemies* (vol. 2) (London: Routledge), 19.
7. In the spirit of Popper's view, I propose to distinguish between two kinds of definitions: a "closed definition" and an "open definition." A close definition is a narrow concept that limits the discussion upon the very essence of the phenomenon and the social problems it encompassed. In contrast, an open definition is a broad and general notion intended to provide a basic orientation upon the territory of the discussion. My definition of manipulation will be an open one.
8. This methodology is consistent with Karl Popper's view that it is quite common to open a critical discussion upon a social phenomenon with the presentation of an analytical model. According to Popper, explanatory theories in the social sciences always, or nearly always, are analytical and model-based. They operate "by the method of constructing typical situations or conditions—that is, by the method of constructing models... And the 'models' of the theoretical social sciences are essentially descriptions or reconstructions of typical social situations." Hedstrom, P., R. Swedberg, and L. Udehn (1998), "Popper's Situational Analysis and Contemporary Sociology," *Philosophy of the Social Sciences* 28(3): 351.
9. The application of major elements in economic analysis to other social sciences is a methodology known as Economic Imperialism. For a further discussion, see Matzner, E., and I. C. Jarvie (1998), "Introduction to the Special Issues on Situational Analysis," *Philosophy of the Social Sciences* 28 (3): 335–336.
10. Goodin, *Manipulatory Politics*, 17.

11. Ibid., 19.

12. See, for example, Watzlawick, P., J. H. Weakland, and R. Fisch (1974), *Change: Principles of Problem Formation and Problem Resolution* (New York and London: W. W. Norton & Company).

13. Compare to Maoz, Z. (1990), "Framing the National Interest: The Manipulation of Foreign Policy Decisions in Group Settings," *World Politics* 43: 77. "Political manipulation is an attempt by one or more individuals to structure a group choice situation in a manner that maximizes the chances of a favorable outcome or minimizes the chances of an unfavorable one." It is worth mentioning that Maoz's definition is more specific and related to decision-making processes in political discussion groups.

14. For example, Maoz ("Framing the National Interest," 1990, 93) claims that certain political crises require a quick reaction. Policy makers assume there is not much time to develop a critical discussion. In order to speed up the decision-making process and to reach a desirable outcome, they present the data to the leading group in a manipulative manner.

15. Ironically, the correlation between the development of knowledge and the ability to examine reality from different perspectives appears in many fields. For example, the well-known psychologist Jean Piaget associated the development of intelligence with the growing capability to examine the world from different angles of vision. Or, in the history of science it is quite common to view developments in modern physics as byproducts of examining old problems from additional perspectives (for example, Newtonian physics versus Einsteinian physics). For a further discussion, see Holmes, R. (1976), *Legitimacy and the Politics of the Knowable* (London: Routledge).

16. Compare to Goodin (1980), *Manipulatory Politics*, 9: "... manipulation is something which actually happens invisibly." Compare also to Goldhamer, H., and E. A. Shils. (1939), "Types of Power and Status," *American Journal of Sociology* 45 (2): 17: "... in the case of manipulation there is no recognition by the subordinated individual that an act of power has been effected."

17. Compare to Goodin, *Manipulatory Politics*, 11: "By the time we start talking about manipulation at all, the act has been already exposed. But when we do speak of manipulation, either in the past tense ('I was manipulated') or in the second third person ('You/they are being manipulated'), the implication is always that the manipulation was unbeknownst to its object at the time of the act. When we tell someone, 'You are being manipulated,' we think we really are telling him something he does not already know."

18. Fromm, E. (1994), *Escape from Freedom* (New York: H. Holt), 128. I will analyze and challenge Fromm's ideas in the chapter that deals with modern advertising.

19. Erickson, M., and E. Rossi (1980), "The Confusion Technique in Hypnosis" in Rossi (Ed.). *The Collected Papers of Milton H. Erickson on*

Hypnosis: Vol. 1. The Nature of Hypnosis and Suggestion (New York: Irvington), 259–260.

20. Watzlawick, Weakland, and Fisch, *Change*, 101.

21. Maoz, "Framing the National Interest," 88.

22. Trachtenberg, J. A. (1987), "Beyond the Hidden Persuaders," *Forbes* (March 23) Vol. 139 (6): 134.

23. Watzlawick, Weakland, and Fisch, *Change*, xi.

24. Compare to Phillips, *Ethics and Manipulation in Advertising*, 18: Associative advertising "foils the rational evaluation of a product by creating the illusion that it will satisfy conscious and unconscious desires that it may not, in fact, satisfy." The possibility to satisfy a strong desire (or to fulfill a powerful wish) is an important element in a motivating interaction. It can help us to better distinguish between manipulation and deception. I will get back to this issue in the relevant chapter.

25. In this context, Rudinow ("Manipulation," 345) distinguishes between simple and complex motivations. I found it more useful and illuminating to distinguish between two types of misleading.

26. Dworkin, G. (1997), *The Theory and Practice of Autonomy* (New York: Cambridge University Press), 14.

27. Kelman, H. C. (2001), "Ethical Limits on the Use of Influence in Hierarchical Relationships" in *Social Influences on Ethical Behavior in Organizations*. Edited by J. M. Darley, D. Messick, and T. R. Tyler, (Mahwah, NJ and London: Lawrence Erlbaum).

28. For a further discussion on "manipulation in the financial market," see Fischel, D. R., and D. Ross J. (1991), "Should the Law Prohibit Manipulation in Financial Markets," *Harvard Law Review* 105: 510–511.

29. For a further discussion, see Tversky, A., and D. Kahneman. (1981), "The Framing of Decisions and the Psychology of Choice," *Science* 211: 453–458; Riker, W. H. (1986), *The Art of Political Manipulation* (New Haven: Yale University Press); Maoz, "Framing the National Interest," 77–110; Rubinstein, A. (1998), *Modeling Bounded Rationality* (Cambridge, MA: The M I T Press), 19.

CHAPTER 2
The Topography of Manipulation

BETWEEN DIFFERENT MOTIVATING ACTIONS

Manipulation is not exactly coercion, not precisely persuasion, and not merely deception. Nevertheless, in order for any motivating action to be effective it must, at least to some extent, be persuasive, compelling, or both. A basic understanding of manipulation is that it involves a combination of persuasion and coercion made possible by trickery. In other words, manipulation dissected looks like a weird mixture of persuasion, coercion, and deception. Therefore, trying to distinguish between the different motivating actions might help us understand the very essence of manipulation and give us a better vision of its territory. In light of this, it seems that the project at hand should include the formulation of criteria that indicate where coercion, persuasion, and deception end and manipulation begins. But is it possible to formulate such criteria for a clear distinction between the different motivating actions?

Crudely and basically, it seems that every social interaction is a dynamic process combining different elements and characteristics, including coercion, persuasion, and deception. Therefore, even apparently well-defined motivating actions, such as coercion, persuasion, and deception, practically speaking, more closely resemble theoretical concepts that hardly exist in reality. For example, even the more desperate situations of coercion, such as pointing a gun at somebody, leave the target certain options (to obey or die). Therefore, a kind of mutual communication, exceeding physical coercion alone, is likely to evolve. The same concept may be applied to persuasion and deception. On one hand, it seems impossible to be completely honest when trying to persuade someone to act. On the other hand, even the biggest scam must contain certain elements consistent with honesty and truth (at least for credible consideration).

It seems that "pure" motivating actions are more like theoretical concepts, or "ideal types" in Max Weber's terminology, that hardly exist in reality.[1] Almost any practical version of coercion, persuasion, and deception contains manipulative elements. Therefore, the inevitable question that arises again is this: How is it possible to formulate criteria to indicate where coercion, persuasion, and deception end and manipulation begins?

At first glance, it seems that setting the scope of manipulative situations is a difficult and confusing task. Therefore, the progression should be gradual. The first very basic step will focus on the potential demarcations between coercion, manipulation, and persuasion. The second step, which might be the hardest one, will begin to include the deceptive dimension in our discussion. Hopefully, this will complete the picture and provide a clearer vision of the scope of the manipulation phenomenon.

COERCION, PERSUASION, AND MANIPULATION

Manipulation seems to be a weird composite of various motivating actions. This elusive phenomenon is clearly designed to create some of the effects that appear in coercive and persuasive interactions. This observation indicates that it will be unrealistic—and even impossible—to draw exact boundaries between the territories of these three motivating actions.

Klaidman and Beauchamp, who seem to be fully aware of the indefinable feature of manipulation, state that " ... it is difficult to specify where persuasion ends and manipulation begins. Ordinary usage, philosophy, and the social sciences provide no exact boundaries."[2] They suggest drawing a sequence that includes the three motivating actions. Their continuum is based upon the "level of controlling" that the motivator holds at the time of the interaction. According to their description, manipulation, which is a broad concept, moves between two extremes: coercion—a situation of complete controlling—on the one end, and persuasion—the lack of controlling—on the other end: "Coercion—which involves a threat of harm so severe that a person is unable to resist acting to avoid it—is always completely controlling. Persuasion is never controlling. Manipulation, by contrast, can run from highly controlling to altogether no controlling."[3]

The idea of building a sequence between motivating actions seems to be more appropriate than categorical division; therefore, I will adopt it. From any more realistic point of view, however, using the term 'level of controlling' might result in some confusion. In this book, I refer to coercion as a motivating action that physically limits the target's options, while persuasion intervenes in current decision-making to move the target toward a more desired existing option without physically limiting any of those currently existing options. In other words, coercion is primarily related to the physical dimension while persuasion pertains to cognition and affect (the mental sphere). Therefore, any description made from the point of view of the motivator has to distinguish between the notions of 'control' and 'influence.' Accordingly, Klaidman and Beauchamp's presentation, which uses levels of controlling as a criterion to distinguish between the different motivating actions, risks ending in confusion.

In order to bypass that hurdle and emphasize more clearly the characteristics of manipulation, I will suggest a similar description from the point of view of the target. From the perspective of the target, it seems that if persuasion is a situation in which freedom of choice exists, manipulation might result from illusionary freedom of choice and coercion from the absence or limitation of freedom of choice. The last description seems to illuminate some of the mystery surrounding manipulative behavior. It might even be helpful in bypassing the technical problems of control versus influence. But does this description sufficiently distinguish between the different motivating actions?

The characteristic of illusionary free choice sounds like an elegant and sophisticated compromise taken from an unclear academic discussion. From any more realistic point of view, however, illusionary free choice is a vague term that might begin to concretize the illusiveness of the manipulation phenomenon but certainly demands careful examination. Are there "real" situations of illusionary free choice inherent to manipulative interactions? Is the target deeply convinced of his freedom of choice and actually compelled to act?

COERCION, PERSUASION, DECEPTION, AND MANIPULATION

There is a major difficulty in trying to characterize manipulative situations through analyzing the balance of power between the key actors at the time of the interaction. In general, we do not have access to another person's mind. We are not able to quantify variables like the level of free choice, the extent of independent thinking, and the "real" impact of external influences (especially in elusive situations like manipulative interactions). Hence, another shift in perspective is called for in order to gain a clearer understanding of the scope of manipulative behavior.

Once again, like Klaidman and Beauchamp, I will focus on the motivator but, unlike Klaidman and Beauchamp, I will examine the motivator prior to the interaction. I will present the considerations of a rational, efficient motivator who chooses his strategy under ideal circumstances. This shift helps me avoid major obstacles that could not easily be bypassed, such as measuring the balance of power between the key actors at the time of the interaction.

To attain the desired result, a rational motivator, in ideal circumstances, must evaluate the level of control and the extent of influence he has over the target. He, the motivator, chooses his strategy according to this evaluation and estimation. This analysis (choosing the most efficient motivating action) refers to the physical dimension (control) and to the mental sphere (influence) simultaneously, without causing too much confusion. However, this description is not complete yet, since it leaves out one important characteristic inherent to manipulative behavior: trickery.

Morally speaking, manipulation is an elusive phenomenon that operates in gray areas. Manipulation is not an honest motivating action (at least in the sense of transparency), and yet it is also not completely deceptive. Nevertheless, it is common to describe manipulation as a mode of deception—a description that emphasizes certain similarities between deception and manipulation but makes it almost impossible to distinguish between the two different motivating actions.[4] Therefore, I suggest employing different terminology. Instead of using the term 'deceiving,' which is quite a strict term, I propose applying the notion 'misleading,' which seems to be more flexible.

This slight change allows for the ranking of motivating actions according to the level of misleading that a rational motivator employs in his actions. Coercion and persuasion are motivating actions that hardly contain misleading elements, while deception involves almost complete intentional misleading. Manipulation, which is a broad concept, can contain different levels of misleading and, therefore, is located between the extremes.

The Topography of Manipulation

A rational, efficient motivator, disconnected from external considerations, will motivate by coercion when he feels that he has full control, by persuasion when he recognizes that he has maximum influence, and by deception when he estimates that he has neither control nor influence.[5] As soon as the motivator estimates that his level of control and extent of influence decrease he will start to manipulate; he will increase the degree to which he misleads.

To complete this description, I will sketch a three-dimensional graph (see Figure 1). This graph describes the considerations of a rational, efficient motivator who is operating in ideal circumstances. The graph is composed of three variables: level of control, level of influence, and level of misleading. The extremes are coercion (maximum control), persuasion (maximum influence), and deception (maximum misleading). Manipulation, which combines different levels of control, influence, and misleading, is located in a triangular plane between the extremes.

It is important to emphasize that Figure 1 presents the considerations of a rational human being who is determined to motivate.

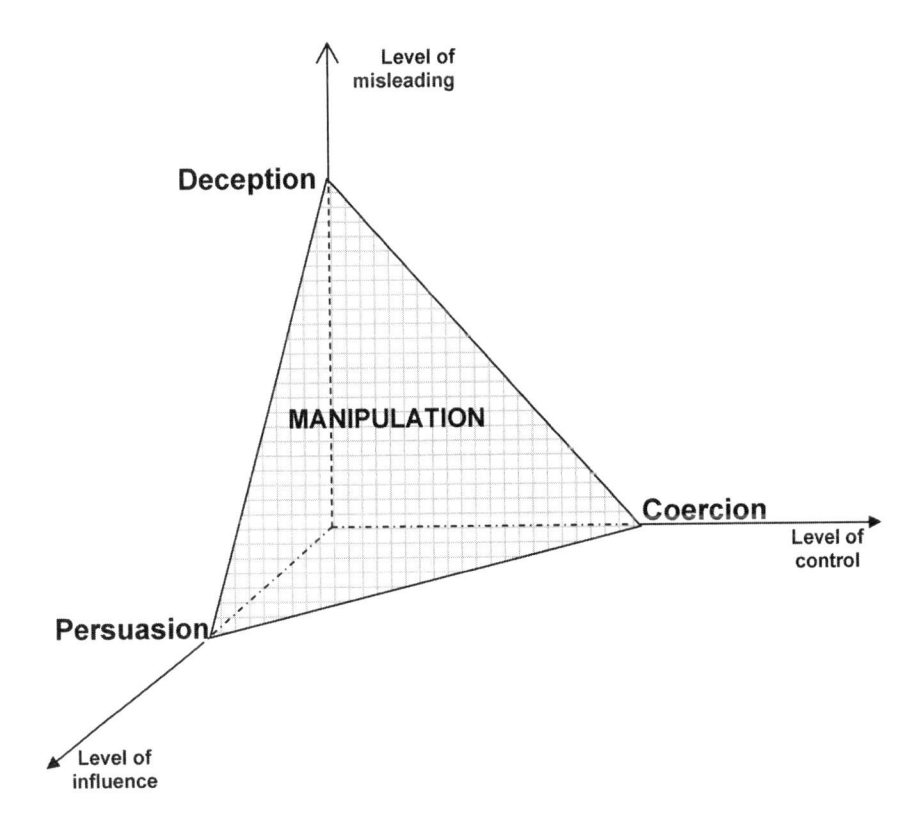

In ideal circumstances, he will select the motivating strategy according to his estimation and evaluation of the level of control and the extent of influence that he holds over the target. In other words, the description suggested here, in contrast to Klaidman and Beauchamp's "objective" analysis, is based on the motivator's evaluation of the balance of power prior to choosing his motivating action. Therefore, instead of an "objective" description that uses variables that seems to be immeasurable (such as level of influence and control in practice), I suggest analysis based on the intention, evaluation, and estimation of a rational motivator.[6]

To animate and concretize our theoretical model, I will ask assistance from an expert on manipulative matters. I will invite Niccolo Machiavelli, the great Italian thinker, to join our exploration. Machiavelli's most famous political treatise is *The Prince*, which was composed almost 500 years ago. *The Prince* is a short political treatise written as a handbook for the common authoritarian leader who has graduated from the academy of crime with honor.

In *The Prince*, Machiavelli patiently explains to his ruler that he has to use force, guile, and stratagem wisely to survive politically:

"You must, therefore, know that there are two means of fighting: one according to the laws, the other with force; the first way is proper to man, the second to beasts; but because the first, in many cases, is not sufficient, it becomes necessary to have recourse to the second. Therefore, a prince must know how to use wisely the natures of the beast and the man ... and the one without the other cannot endure.

Since, then, a prince must know how to make good use of the nature of the beast, he should choose from among the beasts the fox and the lion; for the lion cannot defend itself from traps and the fox cannot protect itself from wolves. It is therefore necessary to be a fox in order to recognize the traps and a lion in order to frighten the wolves."[7]

In our description, the sophisticated motivator will act like a lion (coercion) whenever he assumes that he is able to control the situation. He will operate as an honest human being (persuasion) whenever he thinks that he is able to influence his target. However, as soon as he feels that he loses control and influence he will have to start behaving like a fox (manipulation).

BETWEEN MANIPULATION AND DECEPTION

The last section presented a theoretical model. It described the decision-making process of a rational manipulator who chooses his actions under ideal circumstances. The intention was to provide a better orientation of the topography of manipulation relative to other motivating actions (i.e., persuasion, coercion, and deception). No doubt the distinction between manipulation and deception, which perhaps still seems to lack clarity, needs better clarification.

Manipulation is characterized by acts of leading astray. Therefore, distinguishing between manipulation and deception is difficult and not always possible. Two criteria could be useful in differentiating between deception and certain kinds of manipulation. The first criterion relates to the use of false information in order to encourage the target toward a desirable action. The second entails motivating by a wish that clearly cannot be fulfilled. I will argue that a motivating action that fills at least one of these criteria would be better categorized as deception rather than as manipulation.

Manipulation is an indirect motivating action. This means that manipulative behavior, in general, is designed to invisibly interfere with the decision-making process of the target. The sophisticated manipulator affects the target's critical capacity and provides him with incentives to act. Motivating someone to operate by using false information seems to be a more direct approach. The liar simply misleads the target. These cases miss the unique sophistication of manipulation and appear instead to be clear cases of deception.

We saw that an effective motivating technique is to create a link between the intentional action (the manipulator's goal) and the fulfillment of the target's powerful wish (or the satisfaction of his strongest desires). Often enough, however, the sophisticated manipulator does not specifically promise, or explicitly commit, to satisfy the target's wish (that, ironically, sometimes he, the manipulator, has created). He uses elusive language, such as symbols, hints, and indirect messages, to give the impression that a realistic possibility of achieving satisfaction exists. No one promises us that drinking Coca-Cola will make us attractive, desirable sex symbols like the models used in the soft drink maker's advertisements.

Of course, we can always find cases where the manipulator is actually committed to fulfilling the target's wish. However, in those cases there are almost always hidden elements that the manipulator does not share with his targets—otherwise, there is no manipulation. Take, for example, an advertisement that introduces a powerful, efficient, and effective vaccination. The ad describes in detail the horrible symptoms of the relevant disease. However, the creative advertiser "forgets" to mention that he is speaking about an extremely rare illness.

Motivating a person to act by using a false wish, a wish that clearly will not be fulfilled, seems to bypass the elusive magical characteristic of manipulation. Therefore, I am inclined to classify those cases, at least in this book, as deception. Let me explain by using an example taken from the handbook of the ultimate Casanova.

Joseph invites Natalie to his apartment to hear him play the piano. Joseph, who finds Natalie very attractive, has hidden intentions (a covert agenda) that extend far beyond playing private serenades. There is a realistic possibility that Joseph will be able to fulfill the motivating wish (private concert exclusively for Natalie) only if he knows how to play the piano and if there is a piano in his apartment. In this case we can categorize Joseph's behavior as manipulative. However, if he cannot play the piano, or there is no piano in his apartment, then his behavior can instead be categorized as deception.

The fulfillment of a powerful wish is a prominent motif in manipulation and illusion. Accordingly, it is not surprising to find out that our criterion used to distinguish between manipulation and deception (the possibility to fulfill the motivating wish) is similar to Freud's principle of differentiation between illusion and false idea (delusion): "What is characteristic of illusions is that they are derived from human wishes. In this respect they come near to the psychiatric delusions. But they differ from them, too, apart from the more complicated structure of delusions. In the case of delusion, we emphasize as essential their being in contradiction with reality. Illusions need not necessarily be false—that is to say, unrealizable or in contradiction to reality. For instance, a middle-class girl may have the illusion that a prince will come and marry her. This is possible; and a few of such cases have occurred... Examples of illusions which have proved true are not easy to find..."[8] In a similar mode, I have proposed to make a distinction between manipulation and deception.

NOTES

1. Compare to Weber, M. (1949), *The Methodology of the Social Sciences* (Illinois: The Free Press of Glencoe), 93: Ideal-type is "a conceptual

construct (Gedankenbild) which is neither historical reality nor even the "true" reality. It is even less fitted to serve as a schema under which a real situation or action is to be subsumed as one instance. It has the significance of a purely ideal limiting concept with which the real situation or action is compared and surveyed for the explication of certain of its significant components."

2. Klaidman, S., and T. L. Beauchamp (1987), *The Virtuous Journalist* (New York: Oxford University Press), 187.

3. Ibid., 183.

4. See, for example, Goodin, R. E. (1980), *Manipulatory Politics* (New Haven and London: Yale University Press), 19.

5. I have argued and demonstrated, in the beginning of the chapter, that coercion, persuasion, and deception, are better regarded as ideal types (at least for our purposes).

6. The chief purpose of this chapter is to demarcate the territory of manipulative behavior. However, as it is quite common in philosophical and scientific inquiries, it is almost impossible to predict the outcomes [see Popper, K. R., "Models, Instruments and Truth," in M. A. Notturno (Ed.) *The Myth of the Framework: In Defense of Science and Rationality* (London and New York: Routledge, 1994)]. Accordingly, I will mention briefly the possibility that the final presentation will serve as a guideline for an econometric model that might even be tested empirically. The dependent variable (the variable being explained) is the level of misleading that the motivator chooses to use in his actions. The independent variables (the explaining variables) are the level of controlling and influencing that the motivator estimates he has on his target prior to the motivating interaction. Of course, any further mathematical formulations and empirical tests exceed the scope of this book.

7. Machiavelli, N. (1979b), *The Prince* in P. Bondanella and M. Musa (Eds.) *The Portable Machiavelli* (New York: Penguin Books), 133–134.

8. Freud, Sigmund. [1927] (1968) "The Future of an Illusion" in *The Standard Edition of the Complete Psychological Works of Sigmund Freud* 21: 3–56, Translated by James Strachey (London: Hogarth Press), 31.

CHAPTER 3
Freedom of Choice and the Ethics of Manipulation

THE TARGET AND FREEDOM OF CHOICE

We have seen that manipulation is an elusive motivator that invisibly interferes with the decision-making process of a target. The manipulator generally does not force the target to do something but, instead, provides him strong incentives to do so. The interesting question is: Does the target have a substantial role in the outcome of any manipulative interaction or does the manipulator determine it all? In general, we can distinguish between two extreme cases: we identify cases where the target is clearly sharing some responsibility in the outcome of the interaction and, conversely, we find cases where the target's responsibility is minimal.

The target in the first category seems to have the ability, possibility, and option to resist the manipulative interference, but he does not do so. As strange as it may sound, it turns out that the target is even cooperating with the manipulator. For example, we withhold judgment at magic shows and imitation performances. When we see an actor imitating George W. Bush, we know he is not Bush but we cooperate with the comedian and laugh.[1]

The cases in which the target decides to cooperate with the manipulator seem to be paradoxical. On the one hand, the target decides, or agrees, to give up critical judgment. On the other hand, during the interaction he seems to forget his decision and is not fully aware that he is being manipulated—otherwise, we would not be able to find comedic imitations funny. An analogy to daydream or fantasy can be useful in illustrating this psychological phenomenon.[2]

During a daydream, a person who has decided to escape into an imaginary world finds it difficult to distinguish between dreams and reality. The power of fantasy actually depends on the ability to pause discernment of reality. In manipulative fantasies, in contrast to situations of self-imposed fantasies, someone external is actually staging our private show. We often invite a professional manipulator, like a filmmaker, to play with our imagination, and we even label the most successful cases as masterpieces. There are well-known movies, such as *Titanic*, where the audience is familiar with the story long before the show begins, and still the director succeeds in creating impressive effects of tension, surprise, and drama.

In manipulative art, we let someone else lead and take us on an imaginary journey. However, we still have a strong feeling that we are able to determine the boundaries of our voyage. We let artists carry us until a certain point. Whenever our tour guide crosses an objectionable line, we will probably leave the performance or, at least, show a strong dissatisfaction. The important questions are: What about those manipulative fantasies outside the theater, especially those that are not going to benefit us in the final account? Is the target able to wake up, judge his moves critically, and stop going through an imaginary construction that an interested manipulator offers? Are we able to judge critically a megalomaniac speech of an extremely charismatic fascist leader?

The second category of manipulation includes interactions that are designed to prevent the target of any choice but to fulfill the manipulator's wish. For example, the whole idea of subliminal advertising is to inspire people to consume by transmitting messages that cannot be perceived consciously.[3] A well-known technique of this form of advertising involves flashing high-speed sales promotion slogans, such as "drink Coca-Cola," that can be detected only by our subconscious.

True, it is not clear at all whether those techniques are really effective. Nevertheless, stimulating people to act by using irresistible methods of influence, such as subliminal advertising and other mechanisms that are based on powerful neurobiological knowledge, are designed to create an effect that is similar to coercion. Their contribution to our understanding of the unique characteristics of manipulation, especially in regard to the individual's freedom of choice, is marginal. Therefore, in this book I will not include them under the label manipulation.

The more challenging manipulations, especially to liberals, are those where the target is clearly cooperating with the manipulator.

Freedom of Choice and the Ethics of Manipulation

This kind of cooperation, or so-called prima facie cooperation, becomes problematic when the target operates against his personal best interests. For example, someone who must adhere to a special diet is enticed by advertising to consume food that endangers his health. The question is: How come a person plays an active role in a manipulative game without being forced (in the physical sense) to do so?

BETWEEN CHOICE AND WEAKNESS

This book focuses on manipulative interactions wherein the target is actually cooperating with the manipulator. The most embarrassing cases, especially to liberals who emphasize our ability to choose our actions freely and independently, are those where the target acts against his best interests. The question is: Can it be that the target's active participation proceeds from a free will or is some hidden compulsion at work pushing him to act?

A common explanation of this somewhat weird behavior is overpowering incentives. The manipulator takes advantage of human weaknesses in order to generate incentives that the target will find irresistible.[4] Can it be that manipulative interactions, those motivating situations where the target's behavior influences the outcome, are possible without the will of the target?

Undoubtedly, the extent of the target's ability to freely and independently choose his actions in manipulative interactions depends on many variables and parameters, such as objective circumstances, level of knowledge, and psychological state of mind. However, it is specifically the psychological dimension that could help set the range of this controversial discussion by distinguishing between two competitive radical camps: the Freudian faction and the liberal one.

Freud will remind us that it is quite common for human beings to act subversively to their declared aspirations. For example, a young lady may express sincere wishes to get married but has love affairs only with married men. According to the Freudian thesis, it does not make sense that someone who consistently acts against his explicit declarations and best interests does so out of a conscious choice. It is quite reasonable to assume that he is motivated by certain incentives unclear even to himself (which is one of the reasons that he "needs" psychotherapy). Moreover, from the Freudian view it is implicit that understanding and exploiting deep psychological complexes, weaknesses, and motivations might be extremely effective in leading a person to act in the service of aims that he did not agree upon in advance. Accordingly, the art of manipulation is simply knowing how to "press the right buttons" in order to lead a person to act differently than he might otherwise.[5]

It is doubtful that many liberals would accept such a mechanistic model of humanity. Most of them emphasize the individual's ability to choose, which makes him responsible for his decisions, behavior, and actions. True, the liberals will admit, life is not easy, but any human should insist on coping with real-life hardships rather than escaping to some fantasy world that a manipulator offers. Therefore, cooperating with the manipulator is a matter of free (maybe profoundly defeated) choice rather than the result of someone else playing upon human weaknesses. If the target is stupid enough to cooperate with the manipulator, the liberals insist, he should pay the price for his stupidity.

Both camps, the Freudians and the liberals, agree that the target's cooperative behavior in psychological manipulation is childish, but where they diverge is over the source of such childishness. The Freudians argue that an infantile behavior is the consequence of a strong desire. Each one of us has an inherent need, they suggest, to preserve his childhood and stick to infantile habits.[6] For that reason, the manipulator is simply abusing one part of our human nature.

In contrast, the liberals argue that there is no evidence to support this absurd view. They believe the opposite; that many of us have strong drives toward maturation. We would like to know more, elaborate our skills, and enjoy "grown-up" activities. However, maturation is a learning process that requires investment, discipline, and overcoming infinite frustrations. Sometimes it looks much easier to stick to our old childish habits than to cope with real-life difficulties.[7] For example, becoming a good piano player demands a lot of hard work. Many music students will prefer to fantasize about performing in Carnegie Hall rather than practice boring, difficult scales. Similarly, in a manipulative interaction, it is easier for the target to choose to cooperate with the manipulator instead of challenging him.

It is hard to deny that there is some truth in both Freudian and liberal opinions. Sometimes reality is so frustrating that a person is almost compelled to escape into an imaginary world,[8] and a well-skilled manipulator can take the opportunity to exploit the distress and offer the target a fictitious shelter. In contrast, there are typical situations where it is clear that the target is looking for shortcuts or magical solutions and chooses not to cope with difficulties. In most cases, reality is somewhere in between the extremes. The target's behavior is a combination of choice and weakness. Accordingly, the more interesting and appropriate question is: Where exactly does free choice end and human weakness begin?

Unfortunately, it seems impossible to find a satisfactory answer to this important question. We do not have an x-ray to the mind and soul that enables us to examine the real motivations behind human actions. However, the ambiguity between choice and weakness can help us demarcate the landscape of our discussion and better understand the manipulation phenomenon. The more challenging cases of manipulative interactions seem to be those in which the target's responsibility to his role in manipulation is unclear.[9] I suggest labeling this area of uncertainty the "human sensibility sphere." The term sensibility expresses the ambivalence between choice and weakness.

This book focuses on the human sensibility sphere; that is, on those manipulative interactions where the target cooperates with the manipulator, but his extent of responsibility in doing so is unclear. On the one hand, those manipulative interactions contain certain elements that belong to the decision-making process of the target, such as forgoing critical judgment and laziness that prevents investigation of the intentions behind suspicious interactions. On the other hand, human weaknesses, such as a frustrating life,[10] tiredness from the burden of responsibility, and the common trickery intrinsic to manipulation, promote such difficulties.

It is true that certain manipulative interactions that start as voluntary participation in a free-choice game can reach the "point of no return." Those cases appear somewhat as an indirect negotiation where everyone is aware, or at least suspicious, of the other party's intentions.[11] For example, let us imagine a meeting between a young man who is interested in casual sex and a conservative young lady who wishes to get married.[12] The young man invites his lady friend to see his paintings in his apartment. It is quite clear to both of them that there is a hidden agenda that exceeds far beyond an innocent invitation to a private exhibition. Nevertheless, the lady agrees to go. After a certain point, with the help of cheap manipulative courtship tricks, our lady begins to lose her critical judgment, forgoes her suspicions, and lets the womanizer pilot the interaction. Unfortunately, the results are neither engagement nor a long-lasting relationship but a dissatisfaction for her. Who was responsible in that scenario? Why would the woman enter a situation that is disadvantageous for her? Was there a point in which she could have halted the manipulation?

THE MANIPULATOR'S FREEDOM OF CHOICE

The conventional wisdom is to categorize manipulative behavior as offensive. The phenomenon is mainly understood as an attempt by one person to exercise power over another by employing morally questionable means. Indeed, it is beyond controversy that manipulation influences by means that are not usually associated with decency—misdirection, intimidation, and so on. However, is it enough to pass a moral judgment? Can we conclusively resent every form of manipulation?

I have limited our discussion to cases where it is not clear whether the target is acting out of free choice or whether he is motivated by irresistible incentives that a skillful manipulator provides. The question of responsibility, which is crucial to almost any ethical discussion, requires examination of a related issue that is often neglected, and that is the manipulator's choice to manipulate: Is he or she always manipulating out of free will? Who is the victim and who is the oppressor? Is said manipulator truly an aggressor or is he also being acted upon by an outside force?

It is hard to deny that there are cases in which manipulative behavior seems to be a desperate choice that comes out of weakness. For example, the disadvantaged in society may feel that the only way to express their misery or to receive help is through manipulative behavior. This point was argued intensely by the well-known psychiatrist, or more precisely the "anti-psychiatrist," Thomas Szasz, who denies the existence of mental illnesses and claims that abnormal behavior is simply a desperate cry for help. In other words, the weak in society have no choice but to vie for attention and seek help through manipulative means. The bitter irony, according to Szasz, is that it is common for psychiatrists to "fall in the trap," and instead of "really" listening to the patient's distress, to diagnose him as a "mentally ill patient" and check him into a psychiatric ward.[13] In these extreme cases manipulation actually backfires, as the "victim of manipulation," the doctor, becomes the oppressor who operates under the illusion that he chooses the best available option for the manipulator, the mental patient.

Of course, the "mental illness" issue is a controversial and sensitive matter that exceeds the scope of this chapter. Nevertheless, the controversy over the term mental illness in general and Szasz's perception in particular raises important and interesting questions concerning the individual's freedom of choice. I will return to this issue in the following chapters. I briefly touch upon the "mental illness" issue at this juncture only to establish how difficult it is to pass a conclusive moral judgment on manipulative behavior.

Those who revile every kind of manipulative behavior discount the misery and the hopeless situation of the weak in society.[14] True, we should not praise the use of offensive means. However, we should consider that manipulative behavior could be used as a desperate strategy to attract attention to severe social problems and to trigger positive change.

THE ETHICS OF MANIPULATION

As noted in the first chapter, it has been shown that some women will pay 25 cents for soap that will make their hands clean and $2.50 for soap that promises to makes their hands more beautiful. Selling a plain soap is selling a plain product, but claiming the benefit of beauty is also selling happiness, which is more powerful psychologically and more profitable economically.[15]

Most of us don't believe that soap that contains a little bit of cream will make someone's hands beautiful, but we are willing to consider that a placebo medication (that resembles the drug without its active substance) can help cure a sick person. Most of us are inclined to believe that the first example involves some type of indecent manipulation while the second, in certain circumstances of course, can be considered admirable. Is there any significant difference between the two examples of manipulation? Perhaps our different expectations are the result of our own biases and self-deception?

In order to pass a moral judgment we need a theory and context. For example, Thomas Szasz, the libertarian psychiatrist, points out that using placebo drugs in medical practice represents indecent manipulation. Doctors who use placebo drugs are, according to Szasz, simply untrustworthy to their patients and betray their profession.[16] Shifting attention to the marketplace, however, will lead Szasz to change his considerations for ethical judgment. Szasz, who believes in a free trade of drugs,[17] will probably refuse to express a moral opinion on the sale of soaps through impossible claims. However, he will condemn almost any kind of government regulation that intends to ensure the "decency" of our cosmetic products.

In general, we can identify two central flows in the liberal tradition: classical liberalism and modern liberalism. Each school presents a monistic ethical world view; that is, an ethical perception that centers around one specific core value.[18] The principal value in the classical tradition is liberty, which means lack of coercion in the physical sense. The core value in the modern school is autonomy, which means the ability to choose freely and independently.[19]

Manipulation intends to influence the target's autonomy without limiting his liberty in the physical sense. The classical school does not leave any room for discussing the ethical aspects of manipulation. The modern school views any kind of manipulation as wrong.[20] Classical liberals, like Friedrich Hayek, argue that liberty and responsibility are inseparable values. In the marketplace, any individual should be responsible for his choices and actions. It is a woman's private matter to believe soap can make her hands more beautiful.[21]

Modern liberals, like Joseph Raz, argue that freedom and liberty have meaning only if human beings know what to do with them.[22] Manipulative behavior, which is an uninvited interference in another's decision-making, distorts the normal process of discovering, forming, and realizing preferences and priorities. Manipulation, according to Raz, intrudes on the individual's mental freedom and damages the process of self-creation. Therefore, making someone believe that a bar of soap with skin cream has magical cosmetic powers is indecent.[23] It intends to turn women into soap consumers from false and subjective considerations. In general, the whole idea of manipulating people to develop a consumerist lifestyle is necessarily indecent.[24]

It seems that the different views on the ethics of manipulation result from different emphasis. Raz the modern liberal speaks about the intentions of the manipulator, while Hayek of the the classical school indicates that the responsibility of the target to his behavior in the interaction should be a major concern.

The two extreme approaches immediately bring to mind the question of free choice in a manipulative interaction. It would be interesting to ask Raz if the future manipulator always chooses to manipulate from an adequate range of options. Maybe there are problematic situations that compel a person to take the role of the manipulator. The relevant question to Hayek is related to the target's freedom of choice: Is the target always responsible for his behavior in a manipulative interaction? Is there a possibility that he operates under the influence of irresistible incentives?

Social life is complex, unpredictable, and not always fair. In almost any social interaction there are failures and successes and weak agents and strong agents. It seems that Raz's total disapproval of manipulative behavior is not sensitive to the disadvantaged in society, those people whose problems are overlooked and who may need to use manipulative means to get their voices heard. Is it acceptable to condemn any kind of manipulation, when sometimes a person needs manipulation as a strategy to draw the minimum awareness to his misfortune? The position of the classical school is no less problematic. The responsibility that Hayek projects onto the individual seems to be too much of an overstatement.[25] Is it accurate to say that any sufferer of manipulation who clearly acts against his best interests is fully responsible for his behavior?

There is no doubt that manipulation is a multifaceted phenomenon that can appear in almost infinite variations. From the manipulator's position, it can be the last resort of the disadvantaged in society and it can also appear as a powerful weapon of the conspirator. From the target's standpoint, manipulation can motivate by using incentives that seems to be irresistible, and it can offer a sweet fantasy to people who easily forget the meaning of responsibility. The problem of free choice in a manipulative interaction can be summarized by one clear question: Where exactly does human weakness end and free choice begin?

With regard to Hayek, who emphasizes responsibility in almost any human interaction, the focus should be on the target when discussing the moral implications of manipulation. In the case of Raz, who condemns any kind of manipulation, the center of attention should be given to the manipulator. Neither Hayek nor Raz provide satisfactory answers to the question of the extent of free choice in a manipulative interaction. However, my presentation of their respective positions is only a simplification that sketches a biased and partial picture.

In general, the liberal tradition does not separate the ethical dimension from the political one, as the ethical dimension is viewed as an integral part of a decent, stable society. Ethics is an inseparable part of the search for a social order that can reduce the impact of damaging influences, minimize injustice, and diminish many other social problems. For example, Friedrich Hayek and other classical liberals will argue that the free capitalist society can spontaneously solve the ethical problems that manipulative behavior raises. Moreover, social competition is the best judge in ethical questions regarding the relations between people. How? I will explain and demonstrate this important issue in Chapter 6, *Spotlight on Advertising: The Free Market and Manipulation*.

The discussion of modern liberals, like Joseph Raz, seems to me too theoretical. I will leave it for a future work. Nevertheless, I intend to continue challenging the view that any manipulation is necessarily indecent. I intend to demonstrate that manipulation can sometimes help a person become more autonomous and make better decisions according to his preferences and priorities.

NOTES

1. These situations recall the double-thinking mechanism that is described in George Orwell's famous dystopian novel, *1984* [Orwell, G., *Nineteen Eighty-Four: A Novel* (New York: Plume, 2003)]. In this catastrophic world, the workers are compelled to change historical documents according current interests and to forget the change (i.e., to regard the modified documents as authentic and originals).

2. We need a theory of the psychic mechanism in order to explain this psychological phenomenon. This exploration exceeds the scope of this book. A possible explanation can be derived from Fried and Agassi, especially from the parts that describe and analyze Jackson's principles—Fried, Y., and J. Agassi, *Paranoia: A Study in Diagnosis* (Dordrecht: D. Reidel Publishing Company, 1976).

3. For a further discussion on subliminal advertising, see Haberstroh, J., *Ice Cube Sex: The Truth About Subliminal Advertising* (Notre Dame, IN: Cross Cultural Publications, 1994).

4. Rudinow, J. (1978), "Manipulation," *Ethics* 88: 347, claims that knowing a target's weaknesses enabled the manipulator to offer him irresistible incentives: "I cannot expect to succeed unless I ... know or believe that there are some incentives which ... you will find irresistible. That is, unless I know or think I know a weakness of you."

5. Compare to Goodin R. E. *Manipulatory Politics* (New Haven and London: Yale University Press, 1980), 28: "Man is 'wired' much as a puppet. Manipulating him is a simple matter of pulling the strings by playing on the right symbols to trigger the desired response mechanism." Goodin claims that this mechanistic model is unrealistic. It is possible to assume that Homer, especially when he wrote the scene about Odysseus and the sirens, might have disagreed with him.

6. Compare to Szasz, T. S. *The Myth of Mental Illness* (New York: Harper & Row, 1974), 26: " ... the human disposition to resume immature or childish patterns of behavior, which Freud called 'regression,' is regarded as satisfying a biological need similar to other biological needs, such as that of food or water."

7. Ibid., p. 27: "Many observers of the human condition have offered quite different accounts of how people develop, giving much greater weight to innate drives toward maturation ... All this is not to deny that learning is often difficult and painful: It requires diligence, self-discipline, and

perseverance. Since being a child is, in a sense, a habit, it must, like all habits one wants to change, be overcome."

8. An extreme example of a hostile and depressing environment is described in George Orwell's famous novel *1984*. However, Orwell's imaginary world is constructed to prevent any discussion by its unhappy habitants on social problems and dilemmas in the scope of the text before you.

9. Compare to Kelman, H. C. (2001), "Ethical Limits on the Use of Influence in Hierarchical Relationships," in *Social Influences on Ethical Behavior in Organizations*, edited by J. M. Darley, D. Messick, and T. R. Tyler (Mahwah, NJ and London: Lawrence Erlbaum), 12.

10. It is worth mentioning that Freud believed that dissatisfaction in reality is a strong incentive to fantasize: "We may lay down that a happy person never phantasies, only an unsatisfied one. The motive forces of phantasies are unsatisfied wishes, and every single phantasy is the fulfillment of a wish, a correction of unsatisfying reality. These motivating wishes vary according to the sex, character, and circumstances of the person who is having the phantasy; but they fall naturally into two main groups. They are either ambitious wishes, which serve to elevate the subject's personality, or they are erotic ones." Freud, Sigmund. [1959] (1908), "Creative Writers and Day-Dreaming," in *Standard Edition* Vol. IX: 141–153 (London: Hogarth Press, 146–147.

11. In many courtship games, it seems that both participants have hidden agendas exceeding the direct messages. Both parties appear to be involved in an indirect communication that slides to a mutual manipulative game. I will get back to this interesting issue in Chapter 10 by asking and wondering: Who is the "real" manipulator?

12. Compare to Szasz, *The Myth of Mental Illness*, 139.

13. See, for example, Szasz, *The Myth of Mental Illness*, 119: "This ... is the essential communication dilemma in which many weak or oppressed persons find themselves vis-à-vis those who are stronger or who oppress them: if they speak softly, they will not receive a hearing; if they raise their voices literally, they will be considered impertinent; and if they raise their voices metaphorically, they will be diagnosed as insane." Of course, the case of mental illness in particular is a wide and controversial matter. I note Szasz's radical view only to concretize how manipulative behavior can be a last-ditch strategy born of desperation.

14. For example, Goodin (*Manipulatory Politics*, 22) looks at manipulative behavior as an exercise of power. He points out that manipulation, compared to other motivating actions, takes the lowest position in the scale of morality: "Morally speaking, the distinction between manipulative and non-manipulative power plays is parallel to that between 'cheating' someone and merely 'beating' him. What makes us object to cheating is not just that in so doing the cheater moves outside the rules of whatever game he is playing ... but rather that he is deceiving others in pretending to play according to

rules which he then proceeds to violate. Cheating has as its defining characteristics to 'deceive, trick, deal fraudulently.' That is what makes cheating someone so much worse than beating him. That, too, is one of the things that makes manipulating someone so much worse than just exercise power over him." Goodin seems to forget that manipulation, an exercise of power in his terminology, can be the last resort of the weak, the powerless, and the disadvantaged in society.

15. See Trachtenberg, J. A., "Beyond the Hidden Persuaders," *Forbes* (March 23, 1987) Vol. 139 (6): 134.

16. Szasz, T. S., "Placebos, Healing and a Mother's Kiss," in Letters to the Editor, *New York Times*, May 29, 2001: "It is self-evident that the so-called placebo effect is just as imaginary as is the therapeutic effect of any other kind of faith healing. In addition, the term is an offensive relic of medical paternalism. What is a placebo? A lie that the physician tells the patient. Accordingly, the placebo is not a species of treatment, but a species of deception..." Available at http://query.nytimes.com/gst/fullpage.html?res=940CE6D6153CF93AA15756C0A9679C8B63

17. See, for example, Szasz, T. S., *Ceremonial Chemistry: The Ritual Persecution of Drugs, Addicts, and Pushers* (New York: Syracuse University Press, 2003).

18. In contrast to monistic ethical-political theories that center on one super value, pluralism is usually associated with the idea that there are irreducibly many prudential values. For a further discussion on the monism-pluralism issue, see Griffin, J., *Well-Being: Its Meaning, Measurement and Moral Importance* (Oxford: Clarendon Press, 1986) 89–92.

19. To clarify the far-reaching significance that stems from this difference of opinion, I chose to focus on the theories of two central thinkers: Friedrich Hayek, representing the classical school and considered one of its most significant spokesmen in the twentieth century, and Joseph Raz, one of the major modern liberal philosophers. In this section, I mainly refer to F. A. Hayek's classical book *The Constitution of Liberty* (Chicago: University of Chicago Press, 1960, page 12) and J. Raz's well-known composition *The Morality of Freedom* (New York: Oxford University Press, page 390). Hayek's leading value is freedom—lack of coercion. Raz's central value is personal autonomy—"the ideal of free and conscious self creation.".

20. See Raz, *The Morality of Freedom*, 378: "Coercion and manipulation subject the will of one person to that of another. That violates his independence and is inconsistent with his autonomy." Moreover, manipulating someone expresses disrespect for him: "It is commonplace to say that by coercing or manipulating a person one treats him as an object rather than as an autonomous person." (Ibid.) Therefore, manipulation is an indecent motivating action.

21. See, for example, Hayek, *The Constitution of Liberty*, 75–76: "When men are allowed to act as they see fit, they must also be held responsible for the results of their efforts."

22. See, for example, Raz, *The Morality of Freedom*, 390.

23. It does not mean that it is illegal. Both Hayek and Raz differentiate between the moral dimension and the legal one.

24. According to Raz's ideal, the individual's "choice must be free from coercion and manipulation by others, he must be independent." (Raz, *The Morality of Freedom*, 373).

25. See, for example, Hayek, *The Constitution of Liberty*, 75–76: "... we believe that, in general, the knowledge that he will be held responsible will influence a person's conduct in a desirable direction."

CHAPTER 4
Four Types of Manipulation

Manipulative behavior is geared toward indirect interference in the decision-making of another person, usually without his or her approval. Manipulation is not exactly coercion or persuasion or deception. This elusive phenomenon is located somewhere in the gray area between these motivating actions. The ambiguity of manipulation enables the phenomenon to appear in almost infinite forms and under many different guises.

This chapter sketches a model to classify different kinds of manipulative strategies. It proposes to categorize manipulations according to criteria related to sensitive issues for the open society in general and the liberal philosophy in particular. The chief purpose is to create a lexicon to facilitate better political and ethical discussions regarding manipulative behavior and its implications on our social life.

In principle, the open society has always defended the individual's liberty, autonomy, and independence. Therefore, it seems that almost any moral-political discussion under the liberal umbrella needs to examine the connection between the problem at hand and the ability of the individuals involved to freely choose their actions. Of course, it is extremely important in the case of manipulation.

My first criterion will be the intentions of a rational manipulator concerning the target's freedom of choice. I propose distinguishing between two types of manipulation:

1. Limiting manipulations. These manipulations are intended to limit a target by maneuvering the target toward one specific

option or reducing the number of options that he considers while making a decision.
2. Expanding manipulations. These manipulations are intended to open a target's mind by maneuvering the target to expand his "field of vision" toward open possibilities while making decisions.

Categorizing manipulation according to limited or expanded choices is insufficient. It omits a unique characteristic of manipulative behavior: trickery. Of course, trickery can manifest itself in many variations that might affect the target on different levels. Therefore, any categorization of manipulation according to various ends should be cross-referenced with classification according to different means to achieve the ends. Is such classification possible?

The difficulty is that manipulative behavior is a sweeping phenomenon encompassing infinite means, including temptation, distraction, and intimidation. Therefore, in order to cope with the classification problem, which seems impossible at first, we need to employ a simple device. Let us take a close look at the phenomenon.

Manipulative behavior can be quite a sophisticated motivating action that appears in many forms, shapes, and disguises. A rational manipulator, while choosing his strategy, considers several means and methods of influence, everything from fear and intimidation to pity and flattery. However, we should not forget that all such means remain geared toward the generation of a motivating effect.

The thrust is that focusing on the motivating effect "miraculously" enables us to distinguish between two types of manipulative strategies: emotional and intellectual. The first one is geared toward maneuvering the target to act impulsively while the second one is geared toward maneuvering the target to "choose" his actions out of biased, subjective considerations.[1] Hence, the motivating effect criterion enables us to distinguish between two kinds of manipulations:

1. Emotional manipulations. These manipulations are geared toward maneuvering the target to act impulsively, reflexively, and automatically.
2. Intellectual manipulations. These manipulations are geared toward maneuvering the target to act from reason and consideration of some sort.

It is important to emphasize that in both types of manipulations the means could be emotional, intellectual, or both. The difference lies in the motivating effect.

It is clear that argumentation and reasoning can motivate a person to act impulsively. Good examples include "killing" jokes, such as the story about the Jewish rabbi who refuses to bury a dog in a Jewish ceremony. However, after receiving a considerable sum of money, our rabbi suddenly reverses his verdict and declares, "It comes to my attention that this dog is actually a Jewish dog and, therefore, deserves a full ceremony in accordance with orthodox Jewish law."

Of course, the manipulator is the joke-teller while the target is his audience. Under the assumption that a "real" laugh is an impulsive reaction, jokes can be classified as emotional manipulations. However, entertainment can enfold hidden political messages. Indeed, many jokes and caricatures make fun of Jewish people by drawing frightening pictures of them. These confusing messages intend to give the impression that Jewish people are inhuman and, therefore, introduce to the listener a reason to vote for Jew-hating political candidates. Accordingly, in the final account we face an intellectual manipulation: "Jews are not human. Therefore, I shall vote for the leader who knows how to 'solve' this 'bothersome' problem."

The differences between the two types of manipulation, emotional and intellectual, lie in the motivating effect. Emotional manipulations are meant to confuse and limit the target's ability to provide any logical explanation for his actions, while intellectual manipulations are built to supply the target with an adequate rationalization to behave in a way that the manipulator wants. Combining the classification of means with that of ends enables us to distinguish between four types of manipulation, as shown in Table 1:

Table 1

Ends \ Means	Emotional	Intellectual
Limiting	Limiting emotional manipulations	Limiting intellectual manipulations
Expanding	Expanding emotional manipulations	Expanding intellectual manipulations

Certainly, this model does not encompass all possible manipulations. The ability to distinguish between intellectual and emotional manipulations can be extremely difficult. To facilitate discussion and bypass this obstacle, most examples in this book begin in the laboratory of a rational manipulator. I will assume that in each case the intention was to manipulate and that the manipulator decided in advance which motivating effect he wished to create: emotional or intellectual.

Of course, to remain exclusively in the laboratory of a rational manipulator is insufficient because reality is dynamic, complex, and unpredictable. Each strategy, as sophisticated as it could be, can lead to many unintended consequences. The evaluation of possible outcomes and implications in deciphering a manipulative interaction will help me present the challenges that manipulation embodies to passionate advocates of the open society.[2]

NOTES

1. I borrowed this idea, emotional versus intellectual, from Fried and Agassi [*Paranoia: A Study in Diagnosis* (Dordrecht: D. Reidel Publishing Company.1976)]. The authors use this distinction to differentiate between different kinds of mental sicknesses. At first blush, it seems that the two subjects, demarcating mental illnesses and classifying manipulative strategies, are disconnected. However, mental patients are often enough labeled as human beings who have had their decision-making process damaged, and manipulative behavior is motivated by external hidden interference in the decision-making process of a target. Therefore, it is not so hard to find the parallel.

2. I assume that there are other proposals to classify manipulations. For example, Maoz ("Framing the National Interest: The Manipulation of Foreign Policy Decisions in Group Settings," *World Politics*, 43 (1990): 92–94), writing on the subject of political manipulation, proposes different classifications. I do not claim that my proposal is the best available way to classify manipulations. My hope is that my proposal, the model presented here, will suffice as an efficient methodological instrument to introduce problems and dilemmas via the analysis of manipulative strategies and their ramifications.

CHAPTER 5

Introducing Manipulations That Limit Us

"Limiting manipulations" aim at narrowing the target's perception of available options. Usually, the intention is to maneuver him to operate toward one specific goal. I have proposed to distinguish between two types of manipulations: emotional and intellectual. The first one is geared toward maneuvering the target to act impulsively, automatically, and almost without any sense of consideration. The second one is geared toward convincing the target to act in a way that the manipulator favors.

Chapters 6, 7, and 8 present manipulative strategies in three areas: advertisements, politics, and leadership. Advertisers are considered professional manufacturers of manipulations. Politics is regarded as the art of manipulation. Leadership is associated with the expertise of changing and even manipulating minds.

The chapter on advertisements introduces the problem of manipulative advertising in a free society. It presents the excessive view that manipulative advertising maneuvers us to be obsessive consumers without almost any power to object. On the other hand, however, it explains the dangers of governmental regulation and censorship on advertising in the marketplace. It also explores the various motivations, techniques, and strategies of advertisers operating in a free market and emphasizes that the free market does not provide ideal conditions for experimentations in manipulation and human design. The free market, which is never completely free, has its own restraints that limit the massive production of manipulation. However, the discussion challenges the view that a free market system is the best available system to protect us, the consumers, from damaging influences.

The chapter on politics focuses on manipulative techniques designed to shift voters' decisions at election time. It demonstrates how the sophisticated manipulator can manipulate minds, change election results, and play the system. It describes how difficult it is to determine the boundary between fair and unfair influence upon the voter and shows how a skilled politician can effectively use this limitation to advance his political ambitions. However, history shows that not every manipulative politician is a bad leader. There are politicians that employed sophisticated, unsophisticated, and even cheap manipulative strategies to climb all the way to the top, but nevertheless proved to be great leaders. This observation—or more precisely, painful observation—demonstrates how difficult is to distinguish between decent and indecent, desirable and undesirable, and legal and illegal manipulation.

The chapter on manipulative leadership distinguishes between intellectual leaders and political leaders. Intellectual leaders affect our minds through their scholarly, scientific, and intellectual works, such as books, discoveries, and innovations. Political leaders influence our life through their political actions.[1] In both cases of leadership, it is our moral obligation to demand responsible leadership. The chapter focuses on tragic occurrences in human life, civil war and intractable conflict, and explains and challenges the view that in those desperate situations, only a drastic move by a strong leader can create beneficial change. It uses the controversial writings of the intellectual leader Niccolo Machiavelli to interpret a drastic move that led to a turning point in one of the most fixed struggles in the world: the Arab-Israeli conflict. It illustrates the story of Anwar Sadat, the former president of Egypt, and his diplomatic offensive, explaining how Sadat's dramatic initiative in 1977 led to a peace agreement between Egypt and Israel. This striking story helps demonstrate one of Machiavelli's most basic rules: that not every subversive political manipulation is morally inappropriate.

My hope is that a multidimensional exploration of advertising, politics, and leadership will give the reader a broad overview on "limiting manipulations" and the challenges that they hold to believers in a free, liberal society.

NOTE

1. Gardner, H., *Changing Minds: The Art and Science of Changing Our Own and Other People's Minds* (Boston: Harvard Business School Press, 2006).

CHAPTER 6

Spotlight on Advertising: The Free Market and Manipulation

HYPNOSIS, COMPETITION, AND MANIPULATIONS

One need not be a professional to notice the distance between the practical functionality of material goods and the strategies used to sell them. Modern advertising is mainly focused on drawing associations from the physical qualities of products to the unfulfilled yearnings of potential consumers. These methods of influence qualify as manipulation.

Such an analysis of modern advertising techniques was emphasized and stretched almost to its limits by members of "the Frankfurt school of political thought." Particularly, Erich Fromm, one of the prominent figures of the Frankfurt school who is well known for his psychoanalytic critique of society, compared modern advertising's methods of influence to hypnosis:

> "A vast sector of modern advertising is different; it does not appeal to reason but to emotion; like any other kind of hypnoid suggestion, it tries to impress its objects emotionally and then make them submit intellectually. This type of advertising impresses the customer by all sorts of means: by repetition of the same formula again and again; by the influence of an authoritative image, like that of a society lady or of a famous boxer, who smokes a certain brand of cigarette; by attracting the customer and at the same time weakening his critical abilities by the sex appeal of a pretty girl; by terrorizing him with the threat of

"b.o." or "halitosis;" or yet again by stimulating daydreams about a sudden change in one's whole course of life brought about by buying a certain shirt or soap. All these methods are essentially irrational; they have nothing to do with the qualities of the merchandise, and they smother and kill the critical capacities of the customer like an opiate or outright hypnosis. They give him a certain satisfaction by their daydream qualities just as the movies do, but at the same time they increase his feeling of smallness and powerlessness."[1]

Erich Fromm's description suggests a clear distinction between two participants in the manipulative interaction: the active manipulator (the advertiser) and his passive target (the consumer). It seems to be not too much of an exaggeration to claim that Fromm draws a mechanistic image of human beings that can be molded into consumers without any shadow of independent consideration. According to this description, the impression is that the art of manipulation is simply finding the right "buttons" to press.[2]

No doubt, many liberals, especially individualists, will never accept such a mechanistic model of humanity. Most of them will emphasize the individual's ability to choose, which makes him responsible for his decisions, behavior, and actions. If a person is stupid enough to believe in an externally made fantasy, this is his personal problem and he should bear the consequences.

Of course, the emphasis on the individual's ability to choose is only part of the picture because advertising and sales promotion, at least in open societies, play an active role in the dynamic crucible of a competitive market. A competitive market has its own rules, written or unwritten, that give constraints and boundaries to the manipulative game.

Generally speaking, the advertising agencies are mediators, usually between manufacturers and consumers, creating manipulations for whosoever is willing to pay. The crucial point is that the advertiser has his own interests that do not always overlap with the ambitions of those who hire him. For example, it seems that, often enough, the advertiser finds himself operating between his client's demand for a magical advertisement that possesses infinite influential power and his own interests to limit the time of the advertisement's impact and thus renew the demand for more advertising (an important point that Erich Fromm seems to miss).

The advertiser, like almost any competitive actor, wishes to create and sustain a market for his services. Therefore, he must be cautious not to create permanent "fixations" in the consumers' minds, such as drinking one brand of soft drink forever and without any breaks. The reason is that such an imaginary success of planting in the consumers' mind the conviction that they are going to drink one specific soft drink for the rest of their life will probably reduce the demand for future advertising services. The advertiser prefers that each profitable campaign will lead to the next campaign, indefinitely. One of the methods to maximize this chain reaction is to limit the time of an advertisement's influence.

The implication of the last description is that the advertiser manipulates the consumer and the manufacturer at the same time. However, the manipulation of the consumer is mainly emotional, while the manipulation of the manufacturer is mostly intellectual. The advertiser, who motivates the consumer to act impulsively and without any sense of consideration, maneuvers the producer to become dependent upon the advertiser's services according to reasoning and rational argumentation: the influence of the present campaign has faded away, so it is necessary to start another campaign as soon as possible. The punch line is that the manufacturer takes for granted the advertiser's human and professional limitations without considering that there might be an intentional strategy of planned obsolescence.

The balance of power between the advertiser and the manufacturer, briefly described here, is incomplete and no more than the conjecture of my own surmise. However, it is beyond controversy that the way from the manufacturer to the consumer's pocket passes through many "partners," or more precisely competitors, that have their own independent interests. My schematic description merely serves to illustrate the notion of "competition" in its wide and multidimensional structure. It intends to give a general idea about the role of the competitive market in protecting consumers from damaging influences.

This particular aspect of competition might sound strange and even contradictory to our first intuition because competition is usually associated with the benefit of a small, successful group: the winners. This perception of competition seems to be very clear and concrete to us: sporting contests, elections, chess games, and so on. In the wide social context, however, competition is a broad concept subject to far more complicated interactions, rules, and constraints.

The perception of competition in the global social context and its advantages and disadvantages belongs to the wide debate on how to conduct a decent social order. This fundamental dispute is reflected in any political and moral discussion dealing with manipulative behavior in general and the advertising market in particular. For example, many of the free market economists claim that a competitive free market is able to spontaneously solve, or at least diminish, the kind of problems Erich Fromm raises. Before introducing solutions such as free competition, however, it is first necessary to formulate problems and dilemmas concerning the influence of modern advertising on the course of our life. Therefore, I will come back to this important issue in more detail in the last section of this chapter.

ON THE HORNS OF A DILEMMA

Generally speaking, the competitive market is far from being a laboratory that facilitates experiments in hypnosis and human design. Therefore, Erich Fromm's description of modern advertising's overpowering impact on human behavior seems to be unrealistic and something of an exaggeration. However, it is hard to deny that many times it is almost impossible to find the logic behind the functionality of many advertisements. We can be impressed by the creativity of an advertisement and also astonished that we do not identify the message used to promote sales. Ironically, our inability to understand the "mysterious" marketing themes does not stop us from being consumers who constantly buy things that we do not need. Therefore, it might be our very ignorance and inability to read between the lines that play a major part in the success and flourish of advertisers who produce those mystifying marketing messages. Let me clarify the puzzle by using an absurd example.

Selling black olives as libido enhancers sounds like a Marx Brothers' joke. Indeed, as Koestler noted, the mechanism of jokes is based on connecting two different dimensions with an absurd idea.[3] In our instance, the key that opens our routine and ordinary life (one dimension) to imaginary divine sexual satisfaction (another dimension) is black olives (an absurd idea). As it is well known, the wall that separates reality and comedy can be very thin. In this respect, laughter is some kind of automatic reflex of emotional activity, at least under our classification (as a "real" good laugh seems to be a spontaneous reaction). Therefore, it would not be too much of exaggeration to wonder if a mechanism that makes us laugh could similarly encourage us to buy.

In any case, it is easy to assume that black olive growers will not object to us gladly buying their product, and for us, the consumers, it is much more fun to buy out of entertainment. Still, the more serious riddle remains: Are such "amusing" and "irrational" strategies effective and profitable?

Trying to sell physical goods by attacking or even creating mental deprivations seems to be synonymous with producing artificial demands. To put it differently, manipulative advertising is designed to disturb the rational evaluation of a product by creating the illusion that the product can satisfy desires that it probably cannot.[4] In our previous example, the advertiser is simply trying to take advantage of a person's depressed sex life in order to turn him into a fanatical consumer of black olives.

Milton Friedman, the well-known economist, argues that employing Erich Fromm's psychological techniques is inconsistent with the basic rules of the competitive market: supply, demand, and maximizing profits. In a competitive market, Friedman argues, it is more useful, effective, and profitable to approach "real needs" than create artificial demands. He believes there is not much economic sense in using Erich Fromm's irrational methods of influence.[5]

In spite of Friedman's economic calculations, however, many times it is hard to find a direct relationship between the physical functionality of goods and their appearance in advertisements. For example, the connection between soft drinks and eternal youth, as is the latent message of many advertisements, is not valid. Nevertheless, it seems that this irrational claim, which has held for so many years, is quite profitable for certain soft drinks companies.

Professor Friedman, who is not blind, notes that even if certain advertisements indeed manufacture "artificial wants," at least to certain level it is always necessary to compare alternatives for dealing with this issue. The alternatives at stake are free advertising and advertising that is under governmental control. According to Friedman, the first alternative is out of a bad lot, and the second one is a complete disaster.[6]

ADVERTISEMENTS, REGULATION, AND DECENT SOCIETY

The controversy over the regulation of advertising in a modern economy is part of a wider dispute concerning the question of how to conduct a decent, stable society. Erich Fromm and Milton Friedman come from two competitive traditions. Fromm's ideas are rooted in the socialist Frankfurt school, while Friedman believes in a capitalist society conducted as a free, competitive market. The capitalist approach is more relevant and more dominant at the present time. Therefore, I focus most of my attention on the liberal side of the social-political map, but without ignoring criticism from the left.

When discussing capitalism, it is almost inevitable that Friedrich August von Hayek—a well-known proponent of the free market system—will be mentioned. Hayek's work is identified with the rebirth of classical liberalism in the twentieth century, and his polemical treatise, *The Road to Serfdom*[7], is a watershed in the debate over the question how to construct the foundations of a good society. This short political pamphlet contributed to the shift in attention from modern socialism, the rational conduct of society, to capitalism, the free market system.[8]

The most severe social issues in the beginning of the twentieth century were the rise and flourish of totalitarian regimes. Towards the middle of this century, the most critical problems were encompassed under the following questions: How does a society prevent the resurgence of tyranny? How it is possible to stop manipulative, vicious demagogues from gaining popular support and public appealing? How does society prevent the repetition of the same mistakes?

Around the end of World War II, the intellectual mainstream, including the likes of the well-known sociologist Karl Mannheim, was occupied in searching for rational ways to prevent such social crises. The core of the scholars, who overestimated human intellectual power, believed in the possibility of creating a better world by the rational constructing and marshalling of society. They were entrenched in the utopian belief that every social problem can be solved rationally. Modern socialism, defined as the rational planning of society, became the ultimate alternative to fascism, while capitalism became vilified as almost synonymous with the tyranny of capitalists.[9] Hayek's work provides a conclusive attack on the socialist paradigm while laying the foundation for an opposing capitalist vision.

Hayek's political philosophy is extremely important with regard to the study of manipulative behavior, this mysterious and elusive phenomenon. Aside from Hayek's struggle against fascism, his thought provides the theoretical background to limit governmental regulation in general and to block regulation without objective criteria in particular. (There is no objective test to quantify the damages of manipulative influences.) Based on his theoretical framework, his followers were able to argue that regulation according to abstract criteria, or more precisely regulation without an objective standard, is likely to develop into unlimited regulation that endangers liberty.

Before proceeding to the discussion on regulation in the advertising market, I briefly sketch a necessary general background that is intended to clarify the basic ideas behind the extreme suspicions of Hayek, Friedman, and other protagonists of the free market system regarding government regulation in the murky area that manipulation in general and advertising in particular operate.

LIBERTY, RESPONSIBILITY, AND "MENTAL FREEDOM"

Hayek's political thought turns on the dichotomous distinction between two spheres: the mental dimension and the physical one. Generally speaking, thoughts and feelings are personal to each individual, while the worldly domain is common to everybody. To sharpen this distinction, I propose labeling the mental or cognitive sphere the subjective world and the physical dimension the objective world.

We can say that every person recognizes two worlds, each of them subject to different sets of rules and mainly dissimilar terminology. We observe, examine, and analyze the objective framework in terms of substance and energy, while the subjective system is subject to principles that we do not fully understand. (Part of the reason is that we do not identify the mental world in terms of substance and energy.)[10] Therefore, using terms from the material world to describe the mental one—mental blocks, airhead, and brain freeze, for example—is meaningless unless we regard them as metaphors. This is consistent with Hayek's view on the term "mental freedom," or as he calls it, "inner freedom."[11]

According to Hayek, freedom has only one meaning—lack of coercion.[12] The term belongs to the physical sphere and not to the mental one, which is, of course, connected to a different frame of terminology. The practical meaning is that choices or decisions, in the mental meaning, might be subject to influence but definitely not to coercion. Therefore, "coercion of thoughts" might be a metaphor, but literally it is a meaningless sentence. Accordingly, putting manipulation and coercion in the same category is confusing and valueless.[13] The severe result is that muddling terms, such as "coercion of thought" or "subject the will," encourage individuals not to take responsibility for their lives and decisions. Such terms indicate that people have limited ability to oppose external influences like manipulative behavior—an assertion that, according to Hayek, is not true.[14]

Hayek emphasizes that freedom and responsibility are connected values.[15] In other words, freedom without responsibility is an empty notion. If a person chooses to be maneuvered by manipulative tricks, this is his personal problem and he has to bear the consequences. However, this simplification of Hayek's view is only the beginning.

Hayek's arguments point out that raising questions and problems, which belong to the individual mental private sphere, encourage the literal interpretation of metaphors. Such mistaken interpretations can lead to miserable consequences, which endanger the foundation of an individual's personal responsibility. The concrete danger is that meaningless terms, such as "mental freedom," will become guiding principles for regulation, and sketching policy according to meaningless principles removes any barrier and limitation. In this respect, the manipulation phenomenon, our case study, demonstrates the danger and the difficulties.

ORWELL'S THOUGHT POLICE: FEAR-PROVOKING DELUSION OR A REAL DANGER?

Social life is not always amusing but rather too often invites crises, difficulties, and problems. The frequent call for government intervention in response to social distresses should come as little surprise. Unfortunately, we tend to forget that governments and leaders should not be trusted. Their ability to cope with social crises is limited, particularly when focusing on the gray area, the location of manipulative behavior. How could leaders protect our "mental freedom," the abstract individual domain, which cannot be demarcated by concrete physical criteria?

Manipulative behavior in general and advertising in particular operate in the mental domain. They are geared toward influencing the decision-making process of the target without physically and overtly limiting his options. Moral and legal discussions regarding manipulative behavior is problematic because of our limited ability to formulate an objective test to quantify the impact of such influences on a person's decision-making process. How it is possible to determine a concrete mental sphere, a place where manipulations are not able to enter?

Aware of this limitation, advertisers direct most of their work at the gray area—the place where it is almost impossible to measure interference in our independence and free choice. Their elusive and sophisticated strategies make it almost impossible to formulate objective criteria to distinguish between legitimate and illegitimate and moral and immoral manipulation. How can we protect the individual from damaging influences that we cannot measure, quantify, and sometimes even identify?

No doubt that the call for government intervention and control in the advertising market expresses sincere wishes to cope with real social issues, such as the desire to reduce the negative impact of irresistible influences, bring social justice, and improve quality of life. Free-market economists like Milton Friedman and Friedrich Hayek, however, will argue that governmental regulation and control in the gray area (the mental dimension) is not practical and will bring only social misery: What are the criteria to distinguish between a decent and an indecent advertisement? How can we decide which political candidate is a dangerous, manipulative demagogue and which is a true social reformer? Which political campaign expresses sincere intentions to bring a desirable change and which only uses attractive manipulative slogans to get elected?

The problem is that even the most "professional" regulators with the best intentions lack any X-ray into the mind and soul. This very gap indicates that almost any regulation in this area is subject to guesswork and the regulator's arbitrary personal view and judgment. The sad result is that such a clumsy regulation will probably fail while the social problems, still unsolved, are only exacerbated. The danger is that the growing pressure for solutions will lead to stronger and tighter regulation.[16] In the absence of an objective criteria to set the boundaries to such regulation, sooner or later we might found ourselves living under the supervision of Orwell's thought police.[17]

This dark vision sounds like an imaginary nightmare, but some famous scholars, such as Thomas Szasz, insist that just such a dystopia—the opposite of utopia—is an actual danger. Unfortunately, some members of our society even experience it firsthand in everyday life.

MENTAL ILLNESS, MANIPULATION, AND THE THERAPEUTIC STATE

Thomas Szasz is a libertarian psychiatrist who practices the ethics of psychology and sees himself as Hayek's student. He demonstrated the previous "Orwellian" dark vision in his sharp and brilliant critique of the very term "mental illness."[18] According to Szasz, illness is a physical state of the body. To be more specific, it describes the body as a broken machine. Just as insufficient water in the radiator will cause the engine of an automobile to overheat, the flu will weaken the human immune system and cause a fever. Accordingly, Szasz believes that medical terms such as "mental illness," which describes the health of the psyche, should be regarded as metaphors and not be interpreted literally.

Szasz points out that mental illness is a metaphor from the material world (illness viewed as a broken machine) that is borrowed to describe a mental state. The disaster is that many people, especially mental doctors like Freud, tend to forget that mental illness is only a metaphor and come to regard it far too literally. Taking the term mental illness as literally true leads to a phenomenon labeled "psychiatric imperialism." It began by labeling the neurotic as sick. Next came the pretender, or in medical terms the "malingering," so labeled because his medical condition seemed much more severe because its cause seemed to be buried much deeper in his psyche.[19] Of course, the inevitable end to this endless mode of labeling is that we are all crazy and need some kind of "mental surgery."[20] The truth is that no one, including "mental doctors," is endowed with an X-ray to test the "medical" condition of our psyche.

The phenomenon of psychiatric imperialism, according to Szasz, turned the modern state into what he has labeled "the therapeutic state,"[21] by which he refers to the exaggerated power that governments tend to assign mental doctors. This power is manifested in their authority to hospitalize a person against his will.[22] The scandal is that no human being, including mental doctors, is able to measure and quantify sanity.[23] Therefore, the decision to hospitalize any human being for "his own sake" and against his will is mostly arbitrary (at least by formal "scientific" standards).

According to Szasz, mental illness is no more than the manipulative behavior of the weak in society as they attempt to attract attention. It is a hopeless strategy of crying out for help.[24] Ironically and sadly, the confusing medical terminology, such as "mental patient" and "mental hospital," does not benefit the poor manipulator. Often enough, the mental doctor falls too deep into the suffering manipulator's trap. He imprisons the poor wretch (the "mentally ill") in a "mental hospital" with a schizophrenic, paranoid, or some other rationalizing psychiatric diagnosis.

It is hard to doubt that Szasz's allegations raise severe doubts regarding the nature of psychiatry. To be more specific, Szasz seems to illuminate some dark corners concerning the moral implications of this metaphorically but thence literally "medical" profession. Nevertheless, it seems to be no less important to consider the other side of the coin despite Szasz's valuable critique.

One does not need to possess a medical certificate to notice that certain people behave strangely, and it is hard to accept the view that an extreme deviating behavior is simply a manipulation by a person intending to attract attention. Most mental doctors will insist and argue that Szasz's "therapeutic state" is very much an exaggeration, especially nowadays. These assertions, whether true or not, do not diminish Szasz's brilliant critique of the very notion of mental illness.

Modern diagnostic techniques can demonstrate that certain deviant behaviors result from physical distortion. Szasz will reply that in this case the patient is ill, but certainly not mentally ill. True or not, the term mental illness often functions more as a stigma than as a medical diagnosis for the treatment of a free and self-interested patient. The important point (beyond the debate on the existence of mental illnesses) is that Szasz's critique enfolds an important message, which is that policy without clear principles might be very dangerous, but policy according to meaningless principles is a complete disaster.

Like the concept of mental illness, Hayek will claim that the very notion of "mental freedom" invites unrestricted regulation. In other words, regulation that is supposed to ensure our "mental freedom" might sooner or later bring us under the supervision of Big Brother. The danger arises from the lack of criteria to quantify damage to our mental freedom, which is a meaningless concept—at least according to Hayek. Therefore, besides the major difficulties inherent in a discussion of the different solutions to unwelcome interference in our mental freedom, Hayek finds major difficulties in formulating the very problem.

Notions such as mental freedom and mental illness helped me clarify major obstacles in thinking about regulation on manipulative behavior, so now it is possible to go back to the issue of modern advertising with much better intellectual equipment. The inevitable question is: If there is any truth in Erich Fromm's descriptions (that is, irresistible impact of advertising upon consumers) and modern advertising is indeed damaging our mental freedom, what can we do about it?

As stated previously, Hayek's view focuses on major difficulties in even formulating the problem (that is, mental freedom is a meaningless concept). However, it is hard to deny, as Hayek usually emphasizes, that there are "real" social problems and distresses that we do not know how to formulate. Indeed, my concentration on manipulative behavior was intended to demonstrate such basic difficulties. No doubt Hayek's disregard of sensitive questions concerning our mental freedom is consistent with his world view. Nevertheless, he is not leaving such problems open. The challenge is to expose Hayek's invisible solution to these unformulated problems.

WEAKNESS, CHOICE, AND COMPETITION

I have limited the discussion to manipulative interactions where the target seems to cooperate with the manipulator. These manipulative interactions have the potential to embarrass many liberal thinkers because the target of a manipulation who plays the role of the mark might simply choose, or more precisely want, to be led astray—a frequent fascist excuse.[25]

In principle, classical liberals consecrate the decision-making capabilities of the individual and his independence. They emphasize the importance of individual sovereignty and his right to harm himself, even via suicide. Manipulative interaction where the target seems to cooperate with the motivator is a widespread phenomenon present in almost all dimensions of life. Therefore, it is hard and painful to accept the view, especially under the liberal umbrella, that so many people on so many occasions want to be misled in a way that might not be for their benefit. Accordingly, I will insist and ask again: Is the "assistance" that the target is giving to the manipulator the outcome of his free will or is the manipulator abusing the target's human weaknesses?

At first blush, it seems that Hayek must affirm free choice because abusing human weakness seems to be similar to mental coercion. In other words, manipulative behavior, practically speaking, does limit the mental freedom of the target, and Hayek has already taught us that such an argument is meaningless.[26] Hayek's opinion, at least as I have presented it, might seem insensitive and even dangerous. Moreover, it seems that a competitive society, where everyone strives to promote his personal affairs, not only does not discourage manipulative behavior but even invites it. It is strange that a prominent thinker like Hayek simply disregards this subject. However, careful examination indicates that it is not a matter of absentmindedness, naivety, or laziness but is instead an intentional disregard.

I do not have any doubts that Hayek recognizes the existence of damaging manipulations. Moreover, Hayek is fully aware, even if he is not always ready to admit, that human mental capabilities are imperfect and that any individual might sometimes show weakness, vulnerability, and a limited ability to reject damaging influences. However, it seems that Hayek's fear—or maybe his traumatic, obsessive fear—of catastrophic governmental regulation is playing a major role.[27] In his view it is implicit that dealing directly with questions concerning the individual's mental capabilities sooner or later leads to governmental regulation, which endangers the individual's freedom. Therefore, such a discourse is extremely dangerous. Issues concerning our mental capabilities should be left out of the political discussion, even if such an omission comes at a heavy social and ethical expense.

The first impression is that Hayek's position leads us to a dead end, as he does not leave any room for discussing problems that are connected to our mental capabilities. Discussion of the problem of manipulation is out of limits. The beauty is that Hayek does not leave the difficulties unsolved. He succeeds in providing a solution without discussing and formulating the problem. The free market system, the mechanism that can build the foundations of a good society, provides us a "mental shield," according to Hayek. This mechanism is able to filter manipulations better than any government regulation and control.

Hayek emphasizes that individuals do not operate in a vacuum but in a complicated social framework. Institutions and social interactions have substantial influence on human beings' decisions, actions, and lifestyle. This influence is mostly unpredictable, invisible, and beyond the comprehension of any mortal human being. In a good society (that is, Hayek's version of capitalism), the problem of indecent manipulative behavior is solved by itself (that is, mostly without any deliberate governmental regulation). The competitive market is able to solve, or at least diminish, the problem spontaneously without the need for rational discussion that might call for "protective" actions, which will likely damage the efficiency of the market mechanism. Toward the end of this chapter I demonstrate the role of the invisible hand—the mechanism of competition—in solving moral problems and social dilemmas concerning manipulative behavior.

As stated previously, the debate over regulation in the advertising market is only part of a broader debate. The comprehensive controversy involves the question of how to conduct a decent, stable society. Therefore, before discussing in detail any "invisible solutions" to the problem of manipulative behavior, it seems more appropriate to explain and elaborate on Hayek's view of a good society. For this purpose,

I add another dimension to our discussion: the knowledge dimension. The knowledge dimension is important in understanding Hayek's world view in general and his unique contribution to the social sciences in particular. Ironically, this area puts Hayek's political position in a questionable light, as the manipulation phenomenon demonstrates the difficulties quite clearly.

PROGRESS, KNOWLEDGE, AND MANIPULATIONS

Most of Hayek's work is devoted to the question of how to build and conduct a decent, stable society. Hayek's answer is that the best way is to allow the members of society to conduct their private life and social life freely. According to his vision and following Bernard Mandeville and Adam Smith, when a society allows human beings to interact freely which each other, under a minimal legal framework of course, a spontaneous order that enables the individual to elicit maximum benefit from social interaction is created almost miraculously.

The paradigm of spontaneous order is based on the perception that in a free market system, the selfish interests of the individuals are channeled spontaneously to the benefit of the whole society. The principle is that private interest is the dynamo moving society forward, whereas competition and market demands are the regulator. For example, the producer that wishes to sell his products and maximize profits becomes obligated to take into account the market requirements and therefore must produce quality goods that are in demand. In this way, a harmonic system that operates efficiently arises spontaneously.[28]

Hayek goes beyond the classical model of producer and consumer and suggests an ideal decent society as a multidimensional free market. In other words, he generalizes economic conclusions and arguments to other dimensions of social life, such as ethics and politics.[29] In order to do so, Hayek brings into the discussion of decent social order *the knowledge dimension*.[30]

Like many economists, Hayek posits that our world is suffering from a scarcity of natural resources. Our existence is dependent on the ability to deploy our limited resources efficiently, effectively, and for different purposes. The practical meaning is that our survival depends on the development of knowledge, and the development of knowledge, of course, opens new possibilities in the many dimensions of social life. For example, many inventions and innovations that influence our daily life (for example, the Gyro navigator) were first developed for military purposes.

The growth of knowledge is one of the vehicles that push society forward, but the direction is unpredictable. The village idiot of today can be discovered as the genius or the social reformer of tomorrow.[31] The problem is that we do not have objective criteria to distinguish between them a priori. Hence, it is important to protect individuals from coercion and crippling governmental control and regulation.

Hayek emphasizes that the acquisition of new knowledge is the privilege of very few individuals, while its distribution to the rest of the population is a long and complicated process. A gap always exists between the well being of those who have access to advanced knowledge and those not yet reached by innovation: "... long further efforts are necessary before the new knowledge that has sprung up somewhere can be put to general use. It will have to pass through a long course of adaptation, selection, combination, and improvement before full use can be made of it. This means that there will always be people who already benefit from new achievements that have not yet reached others."[32] In contrast to the common wisdom, or at least the common Marxist wisdom that emphasizes the destructive aspect of socioeconomic gaps, Hayek examines this issue from a different perspective.

Searching for new ways and breakthroughs often entails serious risk. Almost all research and development requires significant investment without any guarantee of success. As many examples in today's high-technology field demonstrate, however, successful experiments might be very beneficial for the innovators. Many pioneers in this sophisticated industry built startup companies and became millionaires. Surprisingly, Hayek emphasizes that the benefit of new knowledge is the vehicle that drives society as a whole forward because the significant advantage enjoyed by the pioneers provides an incentive for those who stay behind to close the gap: "... new knowledge and its benefits can spread only gradually, and the ambitions of the many will always be determined by what is as yet accessible only to the few."[33]

The socioeconomic gap that Hayek praises might appear cruel or unjust. However, this is a necessary condition for the development and progress of society. "It appears cruel because it increases the desire of all in proportion as it increases its gifts to some. Yet so long as it remains a progressive society, some must lead, and the rest must follow."[34] The extravagance, luxury, and benefits that are the by-products of the accessibility to new knowledge operates in two directions. On the one hand, it serves as incentive for those who stay behind to close the gap and therefore pushes society as a whole forward. On the other hand, the luxury of the pioneers is the social payment rewarding those who had the courage and initiative to risk and undertake new enterprises.

The interesting point is that the same Hayek who so vehemently declines to enter the psychological dimension into the political discussion (the mental dimension is outside the limit) argues that the progress of society depends heavily on a general human quality to desire whatever other people have and we do not. "Most of what we strive for is things we want because others already have them."[35] As far as I understand, this is a psychological argument. If we add to our discussion the psychological dimension, it seems that Hayek disregards the existence of social institutions, such as advertisement companies, whose survival depends heavily on the dimension that Hayek alternately disregards and then emphasizes in essential importance.

To be consistent with Hayek's view means to admit that the survival of any advertising company operating in competitive market depends on its ability to elaborate and improve its "professional" knowledge. Therefore, it is not surprising that the late Amos Tversky, whose work on "cognitive illusions" (that is, biasing characteristics of human judgment) won the Nobel Prize in economics, said that much of his scientific discoveries were already known to "advertisers and used car salesmen."

It seems that advertisers make many efforts to accumulate knowledge of people's behavior and the incentives that motivate them. The purpose, of course, is to use this knowledge effectively, efficiently, and for different purposes.[36] Hayek's way of thinking points out that the advertiser sees in any potential consumer a limited resource with respect to his financial ability and "objective" needs. Therefore, the advertiser acquires knowledge in order to "use" his resource, the consumer, effectively, efficiently, and for various transactions.

The advertiser expends much of his efforts to utilize the domain where the needs seem to be endless—the mental domain. To be more specific, the advertiser obtains knowledge in order to manipulate the target by creating links between physical goods and his mental needs and deprivations.[37] Ironically, coherency with Hayek's explanation of social progress means acknowledging that psychology plays a major part in the success of the advertisement. In other words, our irresistible desire to strive for things "others already have," which motivates us to act, could be suitable for dreams, fantasies, and false presentations.

Advertising is a prospering industry. Its success seems to be stable. Advertisers are invited to increase the propensity to consume in times of crisis and in ages of economic boom. This win-win situation brings to mind two important points in Hayek's philosophy:

1. Successful institutions take an active part in designing the individual's preferences, behavior, and lifestyle.
2. The survival of institutions in competitive environment demands constant development and elaboration (in Hayek's terminology, sustaining success in a competitive market requires, continuously, accumulating new knowledge in order to use resources effectively, efficiently, and for different purposes).[38]

This simple exercise of thought may lead us to wonder: Do advertisers increase the propensity to consume by exploiting human weaknesses? Are advertisers able to design, construct, and dictate our lifestyle? Do they create manipulations that minimize our ability to oppose, reject, and resist their impact and influence?

The advertising industry seems to be a difficult topic to many capitalist thinkers like Friedrich Hayek, as it has the potential to challenge the view that a free-market society is the best available social order, especially with regard to the individual's independence and freedom of choice. Moreover, it is specifically the knowledge dimension, the important dimension that Hayek introduces into the ethical-political discussion, that enables the demonstration of the difficulties. However, a sophisticated and deep thinker like Hayek would not stand astonished or defeated for long, but before constructing Hayek's possible answers, a further elaboration on the challenge and the difficulties will be appropriate.

KNOWLEDGE, MAGIC, AND MANIPULATION

Tautologically, given fair play the participants freely acknowledge, agree, and commit to the rules of the game. In the context of modern advertising that would mean emphasizing the quality, practicality, and functionality of goods rather than exploiting one's knowledge of sensitive psychological weaknesses for marketing purposes.[39] Of course, the important question should be the location of the moral boundary where the game starts to become unfair. According to the first impression of Hayek's view, it seems to be a fictitious problem because a free and responsible human being has the ability to reject, object, and resist to almost any manipulative attempt. But is this actually so? Interestingly, Hayek's perception of the development and division of knowledge in society raises severe doubts on that very score. Inevitable questions immediately come to mind: Does the knowledge that the professional manipulator (the advertiser) acquires enable him to diminish any resistance by the target (the consumer)? Are people who are persuaded to operate against their best interests indeed acting in an irresponsible manner (as is implicit from the first impression of Hayek's thought) or is there anything more?

A short story from the writings of the well-known anthropologist Edward Evans-Pitchard may be illustrative. The story is about two tribesmen who went to search for honey. The first one did not succeed and returned home empty-handed; the other one reached his goal, but a lion devoured him on his way back. The survivor who failed his mission was jailed and tried for murder. The allegation was that he had killed his friend by witchcraft.[40]

As far removed and advanced as we may hold ourselves from the primitive world, we nevertheless face similar situations in our modern world. For example, a girl who has been raped is convinced afterwards that she is to blame for the rape (as portrayed in the movie *The Magdalene Sisters*); the beaten wife who, besides being passive to her husband's aggression, agrees with him that she is responsible for his brutal behavior; the view that the Holocaust is God's punishment to the Jewish people because many of them did not follow his obligations.

The common denominator to all those cases is that they seem to combine infantile motives with magic. The Evans-Pritchard's story from the primitive world helps illuminate certain aspects of this puzzling trend. It is well known that believers in magic usually dismiss coincidence. They believe that to every event there is a reason and meaning. Therefore, the tribesman in Evans-Pritchard's story was in deep distress because he could not understand the reason for his friend's tragedy. Ironically, the murder allegation released him from his bewilderment: "he was jealous of his mate, it was alleged, and so took revenge on him by killing him: he magically had turned himself into a lion, killed his mate and then resumed his human shape." At the end of the day, the tribesman agreed to confess to witchcraft and be punished accordingly.[41]

In order to go back to the main issue of this book, I would make a few assumptions: the accusers have a strong incentive to convict the accused according to his confession, they do not believe in magic, and they are knowledgeable in the secret of the primitive world. Our "new" story posits that the accusers used an accessible knowledge in order to maneuver the innocent tribesman to confess to a crime he did not commit. However, the inevitable question that arises once again is this: Could the tribesman, in spite of his beliefs and even with his limited thinking, object to this kind of maneuver and plead not guilty?

As stated previously, it seems that advertisers use to their advantage the accumulated knowledge of the motivations that govern human behavior. Their huge budgets and sophisticated research methods enable them to strengthen their influence. The efficacy of "professional" manipulations seems to surpass the ability of the target to resist any unwelcome influence because very often the target is not passive during the manipulative interaction but is actually cooperating with the manipulator, no less than in the story of the innocent tribesman drawn to plead against his own case. Therefore, I ask again: Is this real cooperation or only a prima facie one? In other words, what looks like cooperation actually may be the outcome of the manipulator's ability to exploit the target's human weaknesses.

It appears that Hayek and many free-market economists are great believers in the human being's ability to choose. Therefore, almost any person should be held responsible for his own choices and behavior and their consequences.[42] However, this is only part of the picture because, according to Hayek, in a free society the market forces have the ability to solve, or more precisely to diminish, the problem of damaging influences.[43]

Generally speaking, Hayek relies on the invisible hand of market forces in a free society to work out moral questions—mysteriously, miraculously, and beyond any human being's ability to comprehend. My own task is to demonstrate the "magical" ability of the market mechanism to cope spontaneously with social problems.

INVISIBLE SOLUTION TO MANIPULATIVE ADVERTISING

Competition is usually understood in its very narrow sense, as in a sporting contest, a chess game, or an election. In the marketplace we are used to seeing similar manufacturers, such as shoemakers, compete for the limited budget of the same consumers. I suggest labeling this sort as "widthwise competition."

We tend to forget that even the simplest merchandise, such as a shoe, a pencil, or a shirt, is the outcome of complicated processes of production, marketing, and selling, and that there are always conflicts of interests between the different agents who serve one another in the chain of production, marketing, and selling. For example, shoemakers probably negotiate with their suppliers on the cost and quality of raw materials. This kind of competition in the production chain can be labeled as "lengthwise competition." In general, the conflict of interest between the different agents in the marketplace appears in almost any form, dimension, and structure.

Competition in the global sense, from the point of view of the market as a whole, appears as a wide, complex, and multidimensional structure. It is very difficult if not impossible to understand, let alone to describe, the notion of competition in a complete or comprehensive manner. Unfortunately, our limited understanding of the complex structure of competition makes us focus only on certain aspects of the competitive market. Therefore, to concretize the spontaneous regulation and control of the market, I focus on specific aspects of a limited example. This example strives to demonstrate the invisible restrictions on the operations of the advertisers, the professional "manufacturers" of manipulation.

It seems that competition between advertising companies focuses on presenting the most attractive, appealing, and influencing advertisements. Advertisers aim to create the most efficient ads in the sense of motivating potential customers to buy. However, examining the issue more closely reveals that "efficiency" might gain a different, or more precisely a wider, meaning than the promotion of sales.

Like almost every other agent in the market, an advertiser has to earn a living, and in order to earn a good living it must have customers. Accordingly, the advertiser operates in two directions. On the one hand, the advertiser wishes to expand his clientele. On the other hand, he needs to preserve his current client base and keep them from readily straying into the open arms of another advertising firm. Therefore, the advertiser has strong incentives to strengthen the working bond with his current customers and even to maneuver them to become dependent on his services. In other words, side by side with his natural motivation to promote the sale of merchandise, the advertiser has a strong incentive to make the current ad campaign lead to the next one.

The last description indicates that the manufacturer and the advertiser, which are supposed to work as a harmonious team, also experience a conflict of interests. The manufacturer is motivated to maximize profits via the nonstop selling of goods and services at minimum production and marketing expense. The advertiser is motivated to maximize gains by creating infinitely expensive advertising campaigns for those same goods. For example, banana growers probably wish that every one of us would never be able to stop eating, thinking, and dreaming about bananas. Of course, such an imaginary success would leave grower's advertisers in search of another job. Advertisers, from their side, will not object that the growers will believe in their ability to create infinite advertising campaigns, each of which can be influential only for a limited period of time. Of course, if these ambitions were fully applicable, then both sides of the transaction would have been satisfied. Banana growers will not stop selling, and advertisers will not stop advertising. Unfortunately, we the consumers will never have something else in our lives besides eating, thinking, and dreaming about bananas.

The advertiser has a strong incentive to manipulate his customers, the manufacturers. He is interested in rapid planned obsolesce (that is, an advertisement that becomes nonfunctional after a certain period of time). The advertiser wishes to limit his campaign's range of influence in a way that will pave the way to a new campaign. However, we should not forget that all of this activity is taking place in a competitive market. Therefore, such an ambition always involves a risk of losing clients because when the consumer sobers up from the marketing messages and sales start slumping, another advertising company may enter the picture and capture the manufacturer.

As complicated as the issue of surviving in a competitive market might sound so far, our description is only the beginning. One of the reasons is that the relationship between the advertiser and the manufacturer does not develop in a vacuum. For example, there is another pivotal player whose presence has an immense influence on the manufacturer-advertiser duet: the retailer. The retailer, our new player, has independent interests that do not always overlap with those of its partners in this trilogy.

For example, the retailer is "looking to make money not just by selling products to consumers but by renting shelf space to manufacturers."[44] Many supermarket retailers tend to encourage competition among manufacturers for shelf space in their grocery aisles. In other words, the retailer motivates, or even enforces, manufacturers to compete for the visible position of their products within the supermarket. The argument is that a noticeable location at the point of sale has an impact on consumers and is therefore a valuable and expensive selling tool.

Every manufacturer has a limited budget for advertising and sales promotion, which he wishes to spend in the most efficient and beneficial way. Therefore, competition seems to reach another level. The advertiser finds he is competing with the retailer for a decent share of the manufacturer's sales promotion budget. Of course, this additional dimension of competition brings its own contribution to the complex relations among the different players. For example, it opens a dispute over the most efficient method to influence consumers; advertising in the mass media versus marketing at the point of sale. Those who vote for "point of sale" argue that consumers mostly reach a decision in the shop. According to a 2001 report of the Food Marketing Institute, the understanding that consumers can be most influenced at the point of sale changed dramatically the distribution of advertising expenses. The emphasis shifted from advertising in the mass media to promoting sales in the stores where the consumers actually buy their goods.[45]

This observation brings us back to the field of our discussion—manipulative advertising. It reminds us that consumers might also have something to say about their purchases. Consumers may want to have a close look at the product, think about its quality, and consider its functionality, and not necessarily buy it because of a fantasy about a top model.

The struggle between the different players in a competitive market takes place in different dimensions and on various fronts. The invisible hand—the mysterious powers of multidimensional competition—seems to regulate the balance of power of the different competitors by various means, such as power shifts.[46] To put it differently, the competitive market is revealed as a dynamic mechanism that limits the power of the agents who deal with advertisements and sales promotions while spontaneously filtering manipulations.

BETWEEN CONSTRUCTIVE AND DESTRUCTIVE COMPETITION

The struggle between the different agents, as has been briefly and partially described, demonstrates the potential of the competitive market to spontaneously control, regulate, and restrict advertising and sales promotion and indicates how the competitive market is actually able to defend customers from damaging influences. However, the description is built upon a theoretical vision of an ideal free-market system. However, most real-life institutions (such as the market) do not operate as ideal mechanisms. Unfortunately, whenever human beings are involved there are always crises, troubles, and misery. Moreover, we learned from experience that trying to implement ideal visions can bring disasters. The inevitable questions are: How can market failures be diminished? How can the appealing performances of an ideal free market be approached? How can you guarantee that the market will operate in the most beneficial way for society?

The market system operates as a multidimensional mechanism whose complexity exceeds the comprehension of any human being. It is impossible to collect and take into account all the necessary information that is required to make specific predictions and to control all the events in the causal chain. Any well-thought government intervention in the conduct of the market will probably lead to unintended consequences, and such unintended consequences can be harmful to the market and the people. For example, in many countries the minimum wage laws, which were supposed to ensure a minimum decent salary for workers, increased unemployment and hurt the very people they were intended to help.

We face a dilemma. On the one hand, there is a severe danger that deliberate intervention in the spontaneous conduct of the free market will bring disaster or, at least, will cause more damage than benefit. On the other hand, the free market system, like every mechanism that involves interaction between human beings, is not an ideal system. Moreover, competition, which is the dynamo of the free-market system, can be very destructive for many human beings. The inevitable question is: How do you direct the competitive market to operate for the benefit society, but without direct intervention in its internal processes?

Many free-market economists, who frequently search for solutions to this riddle, tend to regard the market as a multidimensional evolutionary system. They believe that in an ideal free-market system social elements, such as institutions, that are efficient and beneficial for society survive and whatever operates against society becomes extinct (the selfish interests channeled to the benefit of society).[47] The question is: How can you direct the real-life market to approach this ideal?

As strange as it may sound, constitutional economists—especially those who show much interest in evolutionary processes—are highly suspicious of the ability of competition per se to solve all social problems. Moreover, they tend to emphasize that a competitive market has strong tendencies to create monopolies and might also bring many other social distresses. Their general view is that beneficial competition can emerge only in an adequate framework of legislation and institutions. One of their main interests is formulating general rules that will ensure "fair competition."

In the case of a simple game, such as basketball, football, and chess, the rules of a fair game are designed to guarantee that the best players will win the contest. In the social context, multidimensional competition has to benefit almost everyone. The practical meaning is that a decent free-market society creates only "winners." The project of constitutional economists is to search for the appropriate constitution, or rules of the social game, that will indirectly steer social interactions to operate for the benefit of its participants.[48] In the case of manipulative advertising, for example, the question is: What is the appropriate legal framework that can reduce the impact of damaging influences?

As stated in the beginning of this discussion, social competition (in contrast to a sporting contest) is based on a multidimensional structure. Therefore, it is difficult, especially in the limited context of this composition, to examine closely the efficiency of the "spontaneous regulation mechanism" (that is, the conflict of interests between different actors) that has been illustrated. However, a free-market system can be described as a composite of different competitive smaller markets interacting with each other (for example, the food industry, the political scene, and the marketplace of ideas). Regarding our human limitations, it seems reasonable to examine one-dimensional competition, such as an election, as a case study for the efficiency of "the general rules approach," or rules that are designed to ensure fair competition.[49]

The next chapter demonstrates that our limitations in understanding the structure of the human mind in general and social processes in particular cannot omit the quest to determine the appropriate "rules of the social game." The phenomenon of manipulation helps expose some of our limitations in formulating general rules to ensure beneficial and fair competition. I intend to show that intentions to guarantee fair influence on voters during election campaigns might lead to the opposite result.

NOTES

    1. Fromm, E., *Escape from Freedom* (New York: H. Holt, 1994), 128.
    2. See Chapter 3, note 5.
    3. See, for example, Koestler A., *The Act of Creation* (New York: Macmillan, 1964), 91–92: "Humour depends primarily on its surprise effect: the

bisociative shock. To evoke humour the humorist must have the modicum of originality—the ability to break away from the stereotyped routines of thought. Caricaturist, satirist, the writer of nonsense—humour, and even the expert tickler, each operates on more than one plane. Whether his purpose is to convey a social message or merely to entertain, he must provide the mental jolts, caused by the collision of incompatible matrices. To any given situation or subject he must conjure up an appropriate intruder which will provide the jolt."

4. Phillips, M. J., *Ethics and Manipulation in Advertising: Answering a Flawed Indictment* (Westport, CT: Quorum, 1997), 18.

5. See Friedman, R. & M., *Free to Choose: A Personal Statement* (New York and London: Harcourt Brace Jovanovich, 1979), 224: "... advertising is a cost of doing business, and the businessman wants to get the most for his money. Is it not more sensible to try to appeal to the real wants or desires of consumers than to try to manufacture artificial wants or desires? Surely it will generally be cheaper to sell them something that meets wants they already have than to create an artificial want."

6. See, for example, Ibid, 225: "In any event, you cannot beat something with nothing. One must always compare alternatives: the real with the real. If business advertising is misleading, is no advertising or government control of advertising preferable? At least with private business there is competition. One advertiser can dispute another."

7. See Hayek, F. A., *The Road to Serfdom* (Chicago: University of Chicago Press), 1944.

8. For a further discussion, see Caldwell, B., *Hayek's Challenge: An Intellectual Biography of F. A. Hayek* (Chicago: University of Chicago Press, 2004), 239–240.

9. See, for example, Caldwell, B., "Hayek and Socialism," *Journal of Economic Literature 35* (December 1977): 1867–1868.

10. For a clear discussion, see Leibowitz, Y., *Body and Mind: The Psycho-Physical Problem* (Tel-Aviv: Honiversita Hmeshuderet (in Hebrew), 1982). I am aware of the illuminating discussion of Popper and his differentiation between three worlds (Popper, K. R. and J. C. Eccles, *The Self and Its Brain* (New York and London: Routledge, 1990), 36–50). However, the distinction, or maybe the artificial distinction, between the physical sphere and the mental one seems to be useful to concretize the problematic discussion on the manipulations that are in the scope of this book.

11. For a comprehensive discussion on the meaning of freedom, see Hayek, F. A., *The Constitution of Liberty* (Chicago: University of Chicago Press, 1960), 11–21.

12. See, for example, Hayek, *The Constitution of Liberty*, 12: "... 'freedom' refers solely to a relation of men to other men, and the only infringement on it is coercion by men."

13. For example, Raz, J., *The Morality of Freedom* (New York: Oxford University Press, 1986), 13: "Coercion and manipulation subject the will of one person to that of another."

14. Moreover, such expressions, which describe our soul in physical terms, give the impression that "mental freedom" is measurable. This confusion leads to scientific determinism, which destroys the basis for individual responsibility. See Hayek, *The Constitution of Liberty*, 15–16.

15. See Hayek, *The Constitution of Liberty*, 71: "Liberty not only means that the individual has both the opportunity and the burden of choice; it also means that he must bear the consequences of his actions and will receive praise or blame for them. Liberty and responsibility are inseparable."

16. For a general discussion on the problems involved with governmental regulation, see Hayek, *The Road to Serfdom* (1944) and Friedman, *Free to Choose* (1979).

17. See Orwell G., *Nineteen Eighty-Four: A Novel* (New York: Plume, 2003).

18. See, in particular, Szasz, T. S., *The Myth of Mental Illness* (New York: Harper & Row, 1974).

19. See, for example, a quotation that Szasz brings in order to demonstrate the gravity of this issue (1974, 44): "It can be rightly claimed that malingering is always the sign of a disease often more severe than a neurotic disorder because it concerns an arrest of development at an early phase." Szasz, *The Myth of Mental Illness*, 44.

20. See, in particular, Szasz, *The Myth of Mental Illness*, 32–47.

21. See Sullum, J., "Curing the Therapeutic State: Thomas Szasz Interview," *Reason Magazine*, July 2000.

22. See Wyatt, C. R., "Liberty and the Practice of Psychotherapy: an Interview with Thomas Szasz," 4. http://www.psychotherapy.net/interview/Thomas_Szasz: "... all psychiatry is coercive, actually or potentially—because once a person walks into a psychiatrist's office, under certain conditions, that psychiatrist has the legal right and the legal duty to commit that person."

23. See Wyatt, "Liberty and the Practice of Psychotherapy: an Interview with Thomas Szasz," 5: "We don't have any laboratory tests for neuroses and psychoses."

24. Szasz goes further than his intellectual teacher, Hayek, who claims that "... the argument for liberty can apply only to those who can be held responsible. It cannot apply to infants, idiots, or the insane ... A person whose actions are fully determined by the same unchangeable impulses uncontrolled by knowledge of the consequences or a genuine split personality, a schizophrenic, could in this sense not be held responsible. The same would apply to persons suffering from really uncontrollable urges, kleptomaniacs and dipsomaniacs, whom experience has proved not to be responsive to normal motives" (Hayek, *The Constitution of Liberty*, 77). In contrast, Szasz argues that "the weakness of Hayek's writings touching on psychiatry lies

in his treatment of insanity as a condition, similar to infancy, rather than as a strategy, similar to imitation. The proposition that so called kleptomaniacs and dipsomaniacs "suffer from really uncontrollable urges" is erroneous and unsupportable by evidence. Hayek here falls into the linguistic trap of psychiatry: he seems to think that because a word ends with the Greek suffix "maniac," it designates a bona fide disease, characterized by irresistible impulses to commit a particular act. Thus, the person who likes to steal is a "kleptomaniac," the person who likes to drink is a "dipsomaniac," the person who likes to commit arson is a "pyromaniac," and the person who likes his own single-minded obsession is a "monomaniac" " (Szasz, T. S., "Hayek and Psychiatry," *Liberty* 16, 2002: 20).

25. It is interesting to notice that notions like "the people's will" or "the will of the people" in society are difficult to reconcile with the liberal philosophy. Ironically, these notions are problematic to liberals especially because they emphasize the individual's independence and ability to choose freely. I will put forward two comments on this issue. The first is from Friedrich Hayek, who posits that people often deposit their freedom into the hand of a "social expert," hoping to find comfort. Unfortunately, the ability of the expert to ease the distress is limited (Hayek, *The Constitution of Liberty*, 4): "... our freedom is threatened in many fields because of the fact that we are much too ready to leave the decision to the expert or to accept too uncritically his opinion about a problem of which he knows intimately only one little aspect." The second comment is from Karl Popper, who stated that "the rule of the people" and a democratic regime is a problematic combination. The problem is that people can decide to give up their democracy. To fill the breach, Popper had noted that democracy, which is his favorite program to implement liberal principles, is a regime that gives people the right to criticize their rulers and dismiss them without bloodshed. For a further discussion, see Popper, K. R., *The Open Society and Its Enemies* (vol. 2), (London: Routledge, 1996), 151–152.

26. Hayek relates specifically to certain kinds of manipulations in a way that helps demonstrate his broadest view (Hayek, *The Constitution of Liberty*, 4). Hayek objects to "environmental manipulation" that is geared toward constructing the external environment in order to shape the decision-making process of the target. "Whether he is free or not does not depend on the range of choice but on whether he can expect to shape his course of action in accordance with his present intentions, or whether somebody else has power to manipulate the conditions as to make him act according to that person's will rather than his own." Hayek does not explicitly explain the meaning of "manipulate the conditions," but it will not be difficult to determine his intentions. In his political discussion, Hayek focuses on the objective sphere. Therefore, it seems that he is referring to manipulations that are geared toward constructing the external environment without any possibility that the target will know about and object to them. Examples include

hiding relevant information from a target or indecent trading that misleads participants in the financial market. As stated in the first chapter, these manipulations have an effect similar to coercion. Therefore, they are not within the scope of my discussion.

27. It worth reminding that a major part of Hayek's political work, especially his early writings, was in reaction to the rise of fascism. See, in particular, Hayek, *The Road to Serfdom*. However, it seems that Hayek was fully aware that society, and in particular a free society, without governmental presence is an unrealistic option. Keynes's reaction to *The Road to Serfdom* seems to reflect Hayek's ambivalence toward a clear discussion on the limits of governmental intervention in the conduct of society (Keynes, J. M., *Activities 1940–46: Collected Writing* volume 27. D. Moggridge (ed.) (London: Macmillan) 386–387): "You admit here and there that it is a question of knowing where to draw the line. You agree that the line has to be drawn somewhere, and that the logical extreme is not possible. But you give us no guidance as to where to draw it ... as soon as you admit that the extreme is not possible, and that a line has to be drawn, you are, on your own argument, done for, since you are trying to persuade us that as soon as one moves an inch in the planned direction you are necessarily launched on the slippery slope which will lead you in due course over the precipice."

28. For a clear presentation of this issue, see Heilbroner, R. L., *The Worldly Philosophers: The Lives, Times and Ideas of the Great Economic Thinkers* (New York: Simon and Schuster, 1996), 40.

29. Hayek, especially in *The Constitution of Liberty*, argues that a decent society should be conducted as a multidimensional free market. The economic sphere is only one dimension of the whole structure that enables social scientists to concretize general claims about the decent social order.

30. See, for example, Hayek, F. A., "The Use of Knowledge in Society," in *American Economic Review* xxxv, No. 4, 1945: 519–530, and Hayek, *The Constitution of Liberty*.

31. The "genius—idiot" problem has many aspects and formulations. One of its more interesting versions is the search for adequate criteria to distinguish between the genius, who comes with a revolutionary idea, and the crazy person, whose ideas are far from being considered normal. Unfortunately, it is not so rare to find cases where individuals who were labeled as crazy and insane "suddenly" become revolutionaries, pioneers, and, of course, geniuses (sometimes after their death). For a fascinating discussion on this issue, see Fried, Y., and J. Agassi, *Paranoia: A Study in Diagnosis* (Dordrecht: D. Reidel Publishing Company, 1976), 72–73.

32. See Hayek, *The Constitution of Liberty*, 42.

33. Ibid.

34. See Hayek, *The Constitution of Liberty*, 45. Socioeconomic gaps can be both destructive and constructive for society. It seems that the appropriate discussion should focus on the limit between the two kinds. Hayek proposes

a criterion for distinguishing: as long as society is progressing, socio-economic gaps are constructive. Of course, the questions are: What is a progressive society, and how do we measure progress? No doubt that these are complicated issues exceeding the scope of this research.

35. See Hayek, *The Constitution of Liberty*, 42.

36. In this context, it might be interesting to recall Alvin Toffler's claim that entering the barcode into service in the supermarkets has created an ethical problem (Toffler, A., *Powershift: Knowledge, Wealth, and Violence at the Edge of the 21st Century* (New York: Bantam Books, 1990), 102–104). The new invention enabled the collection of information about consumers' habits of consumption without their approval. Moreover, it turned out that consumers are paying twice—the first time in money (for the merchandise they bought) and the second time in information. The issue is that the information collected on their consumption habits, which is accumulated without the consumers' approval, could be used against them (for example, in creating effective manipulations).

37. Compare to Schudson, M., *Advertising, The Uneasy Persuasion: Its Dubious Impact on American Society* (New York: Basic Books, 1986), 6: "The ads say, typically, 'buy me and you will overcome the anxieties I have just reminded you about' or 'buy me and you will enjoy life' or 'buy me and be recognized as a successful person' or 'buy me and everything will be easier for you'."

38. Of course, it is always possible to claim that such arguments are only valid for a free-market society, and our social order is not even close to Hayek's vision of a free, prosperous society. However, we can always reply and ask: Where exactly does the free market exist? As far as observations have revealed, the market is never completely free. Of course, governments of one kind or another always exist and, no doubt, their actions deprive the market of complete freedom.

39. Compare to Szasz (*The Myth of Mental Illness*, 226.): "It is evident, that honest and dishonest game playing represent two quite different enterprises: in the one, the player's aim is successful mastery of a task—that is, playing the game well; in the other, his aim is control of the other player—that is, coercing or manipulating him to make certain specific moves. The former task requires knowledge and skills; the latter especially in the meta phorical games of human relations—information about the other player's personality."

40. See Agassi, J., "Brainwashing," in *Methodology and Science* 23:1990, 117–129.

41. For a further discussion, see Agassi, "Brainwashing," 117–129.

42. Moreover, Hayek claims that knowing about the burden of responsibility in itself will affect one's course of behavior (Hayek, *The Constitution of Liberty*, 75–76): " . . . we believe that, in general, the knowledge that he will be held responsible will influence a person's conduct in a desirable

direction." Therefore, "a free society probably demands more than any other that people be guided in their action by a sense of responsibility which extends beyond the duties exacted by the law and that general opinion approve of the individuals being held responsible for both the success and the failure of their endeavors. When men are allowed to act as they see fit, they must also be held responsible for the results of their efforts."

43. As stated previously, on the one hand it seems that Hayek stretches to the very limits the human ability to choose, at least in his personal affairs. Hayek believes the burden of responsibility in a free society will lead individuals to act wisely and morally (Hayek, *The Constitution of Liberty*, 84): "In order to be effective, then, responsibility must be so confined as to enable the individual to rely on his own concrete knowledge in deciding on the importance of the different tasks, to apply his moral principles to circumstances he knows, and to help to mitigate evils voluntarily." On the other hand, Hayek does not hesitate to emphasize the importance of social institutions in designing a human being's course of conduct. As I will explain latter, Hayek points out that the free-market system operates similarly to evolutionary mechanism. The important issue is that whenever individuals fail in their decisions and moral behavior, the evolution operates to minimize evils and damages (Hayek, *The Constitution of Liberty*, 61): "The evolutionary theory ... showed how certain institutional arrangements would induce man to use his intelligence to the best effect and how institutions could be framed so that bad people could do the least harm."

44. Compare to *Business Week* (August 7, 1989): p. 60: "To cope with an avalanche of new products, each of which is expensive to handle and stock, retailers began imposing fees called slotting allowances. At first, they simply hoped to recoup some of their costs and discourage frivolous new products. But the eagerness with which many large companies ponied up taught retailers a lesson: Their shelf space is valuable real estate. So, producers say, stores increasingly are looking to make money not just by selling products to consumers but by renting shelf space to manufacturers."

45. This report, which includes statistical data, deals with slotting allowances—the payments suppliers pay distributors for "product placement on the store shelves." The report points out that a noticeable place on the shelf incurs high slotting allowances and uncompromising inspection after the success of the products. In other words, this major shift increased the sensibility to the quality of the products compared to the manipulative aspects of its marketing. Compare also to Banks, Paul, "Store Wars," *Marketing Magazine*, 14 (8) 2003.

46. An illuminating example of such a power shift is connected to the unpredictable consequences of the barcode revolution. Toffler (*Powershift*, 97–99) describes a stable control of giant manufacturers, between the 1950s and 1980s, in America's merchandises market. One of the main reasons for their power was their control of information: "Gillette knew when its

advertising would appear on television, when new products were to be launched, what price promotions it would offer, and it was able to control the release of all this information. In short, Gillette and the other mass manufacturers stood between the retailer and the customer, feeding information under their exclusive control, to both." In other words, "by coordinating production and distribution with the mass media, manufacturers by and large came to dominate all the other players in the production cycle—farmers and raw material suppliers as well as retailers." The interesting point is that the power shift came from an unexpected direction. Toffler, apparently, deviates from the subject. He describes an agenda of struggling with difficult problems that seem to be disconnected to the balance of power of the central players in the merchandises market. "Ever since the mid-sixties a little-noticed committee of retailers, wholesalers, and grocery manufacturers had been meeting with companies like IBM, National Cash Register, and Sweda to discuss two common supermarket problems: long checkout lines and errors in accounting. Couldn't technology be used to overcome these difficulties? It could—if products could somehow be coded, and if computers could automatically 'read' the codes." Consistent with the free-market economists' emphasis on our limited ability to predict the full functionality of innovations, "the barcode did more, however, than speed the checkout line for millions of customers or reduce errors in accounting. It transferred power. The average U.S. supermarket now stocks 22,000 different items, and with thousands of new products continually replacing old ones, power has shifted to the retailer who can keep track of all these items—along with their sales, their profitability, the timing of advertising, costs, prices, discounts, location, special promotions, traffic flow, and so on. Now, says Pat Collins, president of the 127 Ralph's stores in southern California, (the grocer) knows as much, if not more than, the manufacturer about his product." Ralph's scanners scoop up vast volumes of data, which then helps its managers decide how much shelf space to devote to what products, when. This is a crucial decision for competing manufacturers who are hammering at the doors, pleading for every available inch of shelf on which to display their products. Instead of the manufacturer telling the store how much to take, the store now compels manufacturers to pay what is known as "push money" for space, and staggering sums for particularly desirable locations.

47. See, for example, Hayek, F. A., *The Political Order of a Free People*, Volume 3 of *Law, Legislation and Liberty* (London: Routledge and Kegan Paul, 1979), 154.

48. In this context, it seems useful to mention the "Freiburg School of Law and Economics," which Hayek had strong relations with. The Freiburgians have argued that competition per se, unrestrained competition, could be destructive for the market. In contrast, beneficial competition can emerge only in an appropriate legal and institutional framework. They employed the term "social market economy" instead of notions like "laissez faire

liberalism." For a further discussion on the Freiburg school and its relations with Hayek, see Vanberg, V., " 'Ordnungstheorie' as Constitutional Economics—The German Conception of a 'Social Market Economy,'" in *Ordo* 1988 (39): 17–31. True, Hayek forcefully argued that a decent society has to follow general rules, especially because of our human limitations. However, constitutional economists emphasize that the indirect intervention in the free market should be more substantial than Hayek's (minimal) general-rules approach. For a further discussion on Hayek's approach, see, for example, Hayek, *The Constitution of Liberty*.

49. Basically and crudely, many free-market economists argue that a decent society should be conducted as a multidimensional free market. In this context, they tend to emphasize that the economic sphere is only one dimension of the whole structure that enables economists to concretize general claims about the decent social order. For a further discussion, see Hayek, *The Constitution of Liberty*.

CHAPTER 7
Spotlight on Politics: Intellectual Manipulation

INTRODUCTION

In contrast to limiting emotional manipulations, which are intended to lead the target to act impulsively and reflexively, limiting intellectual manipulations are constructed to supply the target with a compelling reason to behave in a way that the manipulator favors. The intention in limited intellectual manipulations is to lead the target to use reason and to act from rational considerations. However, the more interesting cases raise some severe doubts about whether the term "rationality" is appropriate. On the one hand, it is clear that the target is acting out of reason and critical thinking. On the other hand, his world view is partial, limited, and biased.[1]

The manipulator is trying to create, or more precisely to keep, a substantial gap between the scope of the target's world view and his field of vision. The manipulator strives to maneuver the target to act in a rational manner in the context and framework of the target's "limited" world view. However, an examination of the bigger picture indicates that it is often difficult to accept the idea that the target is acting rationally, especially in cases where it is not clear whether the target is acting out of a free choice or whether "someone else" is maneuvering him by playing upon his human weaknesses.

MANIPULATION, PROPAGANDA, AND SOCIAL CRISIS

Statecraft is not an easy profession. The dynamic complexity of social life, often enough, invites infinite social problems and various unexpected crises. Therefore, it is not surprising to find political candidates who lack a well-thought strategy to cope with the difficulties, establishing their campaign upon incisive criticism of the present governmental policy. This strategy makes it hard to draw the line between "real" criticism and "pure" propaganda. On the one hand, the critique can indeed turn upon the real failures of the incumbent regime, but to criticize without suggesting any alternative, especially in politics, smacks of propaganda. I propose to label a political campaign that is based on criticism without proposing constructive advice the "manipulative criticism" tactic.[2]

Principally, it seems all the easier to criticize than to offer alternative solutions, especially when there really is nothing to offer.[3] Manipulative criticism is intended to give the impression of a sharp critic who has magical solutions to the urgent problems at stake while, in practice, he himself is confused and hardly knows where to start. Many times the manipulative challenger, hypocritically and surreptitiously, even supports the very same unpopular moves of the incumbent regime that he does not hesitate to attack and criticize in any possible public occasion.[4]

As much as the political situation deteriorates, it seems easier to build an image of magical rescuer, but in practice the manipulative politician does not have any concrete alternative blueprint. Unfortunately, desperate people might vote for a politician who offers hope without examining critically if he has any concrete strategy or if he offers mere empty rhetoric.[5] In theses painful cases, the public recoils from confronting the "critical rescuer" for fear of banishing the little hope that his rhetoric proposes.

The question about the division of responsibility between the manipulator and the target is begged yet again: Which component, in difficult situations of social crisis, is playing the dominant role? Is it the weakness of a distressed people that the critical manipulator abuses or do the voters choose to close their eyes and live under the illusion that the sharp critic has substantial solutions to offer?

The history of the twentieth century shows that the rise and flourish of manipulative totalitarian regimes, such as fascism and Nazism, did not occur in a vacuum. Society, at that time, faced an existential crisis. We learned that the deeper the frustration, the easier it becomes to sell false hope. This painful experience suggests that our critical manipulator, operating in situations of social collapse, is simply abusing human weakness.

Many liberals will never accept this view. They will argue that human beings are responsible for their decisions, choices, and behavior even in difficult times. According to their view, it is much more reasonable to expect that in extreme situations people would take responsibility for their decision making and not fall into the trap of cheap manipulative tricks. However, is it always possible to make the right decisions?

There is no doubt that on occasion society faces major crises. Ironically, protagonists of the two extreme views (weakness versus choice) emphasize elements that seem to contradict their opinions. For example, the common fascist leader, who uses almost any available trick to subordinate the individual, claims that members of society simply want to be misled. In contrast, many liberals, great believers in the individual's ability to choose freely, have described in detail the external and internal social conditions that paved the way to massive submission to the fascist propaganda in the beginning of the twentieth century.[6]

The crucial point is that the fascist's actions and strategy indicate that he is simply lying. He does not believe his own assertion, which attributes too much weight to a human being's freedom of choice in times of social distresses and under the pressure of massive propaganda. In opposition, liberals, especially those who emphasize the difficulties, seem more honest and consistent. They claim that internal and external distresses might be a necessary condition to the success of propaganda, but certainly not a sufficient one. They emphasize that even in the more severe situations of social collapse there is ample room for an individual's free choice. The liberals will not easily dismiss individuals from the burden of responsibility.

The "manipulative criticism" tactic can be very useful in creating the impression that there are compelling and even rational reasons to vote for the manipulator. The motivating message of the "critic contender" is that the existing policy is a complete disaster and that he is the natural candidate to lead society during a difficult time. The manipulative subtext is that not only is the present leadership confused, but that the contender himself does not have the simplest clue how to cope with such deep distresses. Indeed, here we face no more than a limited intellectual manipulation in that the motivating effect is created by a "rational" argument.

One of the most interesting questions is: What is the fate of a politician who uses the manipulative criticism tactics, wins the election, and has to prove "real" political qualifications? There are many scripts and countless examples in global politics in general and in the public life of countries in continuous crisis, such as Israel, in particular. At the one extreme, we find the critical rhetorician demonstrates himself as a failed statesman. His end might be in the gallows or, at least in a decent state, in losing his tenure in legitimate elections.[7] On the other pole we find cases where the manipulative critic is discovered as a talented and successful leader. Of course, these extreme possibilities demonstrate the difficulties in discussing moral-political questions concerning manipulative behavior. Constitutional economists try to bypass the "leadership obstacle" by shifting ground. They do not trust politicians, but they do trust rules and constitution.[8]

CONSTITUTION, RULES, AND MANIPULATION

Constitutional economics is a unique field in the liberal tradition. Constitutional economists, especially as liberals, emphasize our human limitations: vulnerability, limited mental capabilities, and imperfect knowledge. Society, which is a composite of imperfect human beings, has to follow rules in order to successfully cope with a complex, dynamic, and ever-changing world.[9]

The basic idea of constitutional economics is that effective and efficient rules (that is, a constitution) can guide individuals to promote their own best interests and at the same time contribute to the benefit of society. This research program asks the questions: How do you construct an efficient constitution, the rules for the social-economic-political game, that will ensure a decent, stable society? What are the rules that can guide self-interested individuals to operate for themselves and the benefit of society simultaneously? How do you formulate a constitution that can reduce the impact of damaging actions and produce a peaceful, prosperous, and flourishing social order?[10]

Constitutional economists emphasize our limitations that obligate us to follow rules. However, the rules of the social game, which have been formulated under one procedure or another, are mostly man-made ones. Therefore, our limitations are reflected once again in the formulation of the very rules originally intended to safeguard us from our limitations. Unfortunately, the sophisticated manipulator can sometimes function well within the scope of the rules, and even play the system. The chief purpose of this chapter is to show that the rules created to ensure fair elections can yield absurd results.

Let me begin with an example that demonstrates how a sophisticated manipulation can be a very powerful tool. The essential point is that it is not clear if this particular manipulation—under the assumption that it was indeed manipulation—was based on a wild slander or a real danger. Either way, it was a winning strategy.

THE PARANOIA TACTIC

Paranoia is a rare mental disease in its clinical form but a well-known concept among the public. As with most mental illnesses, paranoid symptoms reflect struggle, contradictions, and even paradoxes. However, the very essence of paranoia, which makes this specific sickness unique, lies in one constitutive paradox. On the one hand, the paranoid seems to be extremely logical and cautious in choosing his actions. On the other hand, his world view is established on a dominating mistaken idea, or integrative principle, that he refuses to examine critically.[11]

A good illustration for a paranoid dominating idea is a divine mission from god whereby the paranoid was chosen to bring salvation to the world. Of course, espousing such a "strange" idea affects almost any judgment of reality and, therefore, any course of behavior. For example, the paranoid finds that he is compelled to escape and hide because dark forces are trying to prevent him from completing his holy mission.

It is acceptable to assume that the paranoid is under a lot of internal suffering and mental pressure. The problem is that instead of coping with his distresses in the "normal" way, he has organized his world view in a mistaken but somewhat self-serving manner; he suffers only because he is a very important person. In quite the same way, social crisis, like the Palestinian-Israeli conflict, can be the perfect background to use the manipulative tactic to inculcate the same delusional self-serving effect.

The paranoia tactic is a manipulative strategy of maneuvering the target to espouse a dominating idea as a foundation to his world view. The tendency is to build a vision of reality by raising the manipulator's aims to the top of the target's scale of preferences. This tactic employs a similar mechanism to that of the paranoia disease. However, while the paranoid adapts his biased conception voluntarily and spontaneously, the manipulative interaction is a two-participant game.

An efficient method to achieve the paranoid effect is to "plant" in a person's mind a dominating idea (*idèe fixe*). The strategy is to manipulate the target to espouse an integrative principle that will serve as the foundation for a tendentious and biased world view. However, social life is not a human design laboratory that readily facilitates opportunities to conduct experiments in brainwashing. Therefore, the dominating idea must be chosen carefully; that is, in a way that the mark of the con will find it functional for his life in general and for his survival in particular.

Crudely and basically, it is unlikely for someone who lives a full, satisfactory life to show any interest in espousing any suspicious dominating idea (*idèe fixe*),[12] and it is quite reasonable to expect that he will become extremely suspicious of any attempt to push him outside of his convenient life track. In contrast, the lesson from the paranoia disease is that social crisis can provide a more fertile environment to achieve the paranoid effect. The integrative principle (that is, the idea dominating the mind), which is the core of the paranoia disease and the paranoia tactic, somehow mitigates the suffering. For example, the dominating idea helps to construct a more relaxing world view, or at least shift the attention from the more difficult and upsetting actual problems.

The manipulator's intentions are to achieve results, which are similar to the paranoid clinical symptoms. He strives to fit the mark with rose-colored glasses that can spin any piece of information into the ultimate supportive evidence to the biased conception. On the one hand, the target is maneuvered to interpret any information that contradicts the manipulative conception as a mistake or deception. Therefore, such contradictions only enhance his motivation to follow the manipulator's track. On the other hand, the target can very easily interpret any information that does not contradict the dominating idea as its ultimate verification.[13]

A similar mechanism operates in certain religions, or more precisely commentaries that are intended to promote religious beliefs. For example, any victory of the chosen nation is, actually, the victory of God, and any loss is the loss of the people who failed to serve the master of the universe properly.[14] This powerful mechanism is a "lose-lose" situation for anyone who tries to convince the target to examine his conception from any different perspective.

In the more entrenched cases, the target, who is in a really difficult situation, refuses to cast even the simplest doubt on his biased conception. Despite the difficulties, however, the liberal camp will not so easily discharge the target from responsibility for his actions. True, liberals will be ready to admit that building an imaginary world vision on a "planted" dominating idea is functional for the target. However, should we not expect human beings, especially in times of crisis, to take responsibility for their lives and to confront directly the "real" problems at stake?

WINNING ELECTIONS WITH THE "PARANOIA TACTIC"

A very interesting example that concretizes the powerful effect of the paranoia tactic appeared in 1996 during the general elections in Israel. Shimon Peres, the incumbent prime minister, started the race at a considerable advantage over his rival from the opposition, Benjamin Netanyahu. Yet Netanyahu's election slogan, "Peres will divide Jerusalem," made such a significant contribution to the shift in public opinion that, at the end of a dramatic race, brought Netanyahu to the prime minister's seat.[15]

The slogan "Peres will divide Jerusalem," which triggers deep emotional feelings in the Jewish people, appeared at a delicate time. In this season, the impression was that the Israeli government under the leadership of Shimon Peres, Netanyahu's opponent, was in the middle of a "blind" race towards a peace process. Peres and his crew were not attentive to the unfriendly atmosphere toward the idea of establishing a peaceful partnership between the two sides of the Palestinian-Israeli conflict. It was not clear whether the Palestinians were ready for a realistic negotiation, and the Israelis were prepared for a reasonable peace process. All of the signs indicated a large gap between the grand peace vision of Peres (his "New Middle East") and the conditions on the ground, such as the ongoing terrorist attacks during this time.[16]

The confusing reality, the doubts, and most of all the fear of extreme concessions to the Palestinians formed the perfect background for the slogan "Peres will divide Jerusalem."[17] Of course, this slogan could neither be conclusively demonstrated nor definitely refuted.[18] Be that as it may, a number of Israelis were receptive to espouse this campaign slogan as a presupposition to their world view. In Israel, it is sometimes enough to win the elections.[19]

The propaganda slogan seemed to carry all the potential to influence any judgment of reality. Miraculously, once someone is infected with this insidious synthetic slogan, it works like the obsessive mechanism of the paranoid. Any activity by Peres to advance peace is interpreted as another step toward the division of Jerusalem on the one hand, while any slowing down or even stepping backwards from the peace process is likely to be understood as fraud and deception on the other hand.[20]

Ironically, the question of whether Jerusalem is "united" or practically "divided" is controversial. Jerusalem is the capital city of the state of Israel. However, most of east Jerusalem's residents are Arabs, and at least a part of them prefer to be regarded as Palestinians. Therefore, many argue that there is no escape from admitting that Jerusalem is already polarized. The shining vision of "the eternal united Jerusalem under Israeli control with a majority of Jewish people" is no more than a myth,[21] and myths, especially those that survive for long ages, can be very dear and precious illusions to human beings. Their influence is often inestimable as a call to action in the polling booth.[22]

Certainly, emotions played a central role in the success of this election slogan. Nevertheless, the emotional charge was "only" a supportive background for a rational—or more precisely, semi-rational—message to the voter toward his decision in the polling booth: I will vote for Netanyahu because Peres will divide Jerusalem. The more appropriate classification of the slogan "Peres will divide Jerusalem" is "limited intellectual manipulation" (that is, reason creates the motivating effect). However, the illusiveness of this slogan might call for a different interpretation.

To be realistic, any effective and reasonable peace process between Palestinians and Israelis has to include a serious discussion of Jerusalem's future. Nevertheless, the future of Jerusalem was taboo in the Israeli public debate. Ironically, it was Netanyahu's campaign that put the fate of Jerusalem into the center of the Israeli public discourse, at least for some time. Therefore, we might wonder of Netanyahu's intention was to open a public debate on a sensitive, problematic subject that no one dared to speak about. By blaming Peres for trying to divide Jerusalem, Netanyahu hoped to provoke a critical discussion on such an important and critical matter. According to this interpretation, Netanyahu's strategy was acutely an "expanding manipulation." His idea was to prepare the people to consider various practical solutions to the future of Jerusalem—one of the most difficult obstacles to achieve peace.

Again, the circumstances, the inconvenient political situation for Israel, and the absence of any practical blueprint from Netanyahu's side indicate that Netanyahu used the powerful slogan mainly to get elected. After all, the impression remains of a limiting manipulation intended to lead to one option: Netanyahu for prime minister.

This campaign employs a well-known manipulative prescription of propaganda formulated long ago by Pareto: "To take advantage of sentiments, not wasting one's energies in futile efforts to destroy them."[23] Long before Pareto, Edmund Burke, the passionate defender of liberty, taught us that "no passion so effectively robs the mind of all its power of acting and reasoning as fear." Instead of presenting a well-thought strategy, which requires some intellectual effort from the voters, Netanyahu chose the easy way.

Netanyahu chose to use confusion, fear, and disappointment to lead the Israeli voters to espouse an integrative principle that might be unfounded. By using this strategy, he created the impression that "stopping Peres from dividing Jerusalem" is the most urgent problem at stake. In contrast, Netanyahu, the candidate whose platform was a complete mystery, is the ultimate candidate to stop the disaster.

The tragic figure in this short story is Shimon Peres, the incumbent prime minister who started the race with a huge advantage among the voters. Ironically, after losing the elections, Peres charged Netanyahu with raising the Jerusalem issue at the most "inconvenient" time for Israel (nationally and internationally). By doing that, Peres argued that Netanyahu, the bogus self-anointed defender of the mythically united Jerusalem, actually endangered the unification of the city under Israeli sovereignty. Unfortunately, it was too late for Peres, at least with respect to the 1996 elections.

DISTRIBUTING AMULETS FOR GOOD LUCK IN ELECTION TIME

Netanyahu won the 1996 elections, depriving Peres of any precious opportunity to divide Jerusalem, so it is impossible to clarify if Netanyahu's pithy slogan was anything more than a winning slander. However, this campaign slogan is extremely useful in showing that it is not easy to guarantee fair and decent elections. What are the criteria, standards, and measurements to distinguish fair and unfair influence on the voter? To demonstrate the difficulties, it is interesting to compare Netanyahu's election slogan to the distribution of amulets during election time in Israel two years later. This comparison shows that it can be difficult to draw the line between legitimate and illegitimate propaganda. Let us first explore the "amulets" campaign.

It is reasonable to assume that distributing amulets during elections is not an innocent act. The amulet serves to incite strong passions, such as faith in supernatural ability, divine holiness, and fear from the fury of god, in an effort to guide the voter's choice in the polling booth. However, human beings are not automatons, and voting is not the result of a momentary impulse but the outcome of certain considerations. Therefore, it is likely that most of the people, at least to themselves, are able to find "good" explanations for their electoral choice.

The amulet is a symbolic device that holds emotional value. Its purpose is to send a message with some kind of reasoning—rational, semi-rational, or even completely irrational—to encourage the voter to choose a particular candidate. For example, the amulet may signify that voting for the "right" candidate will ensure good health in this world and a place in heaven in the next one. Therefore, distributing amulets during elections seems to belong to the category of limiting intellectual manipulation in that reason creates the motivating effect.

Amulets that signify good luck were distributed to the Israeli public during the 1998 elections for the local authorities. The amulets were in the shape of miniature bottles of oil containing the picture of Rabbi Caduri and carrying his blessing. Rabbi Caduri was one of the spiritual leaders of "Shas," the ultra-orthodox political party of the Sephardic religious Jews. Rabbi Caduri was well known as the eldest "mekubal," a master of spiritual knowledge that related to Jewish mysticism (Kabala). The interesting questions are: What effect did those amulets have on voters? Were those amulets able to change the voting results?

It seems that these amulets would have marginal influence on the election's outcome. On the one hand, it would have a negligible effect on those who do not believe in the holiness of Rabbi Caduri. On the other hand, followers of Rabbi Caduri do not need an amulet to remind them which party to vote. Of course, this observation is not completely correct, as there are some marginal cases where the amulet might have an impact on the decisions of certain voters. For example, amulets and spells might capture the heart of a desperate person looking for any fragment of hope and he, in return, might "express his gratitude" in the polling booth.

The impression is that the impact of Netanyahu's slogan was much more substantial than the potential of Rabbi Caduri's miniature bottles to shift voting. "Peres will divide Jerusalem" is a phrase that touches the heart of Jewish people and reaches a wide public across the entire political spectrum. However, one of the most fascinating issues is that the Israeli Supreme Court, which did not disqualify Netanyahu's slogan, prohibited the use of the amulets as election propaganda.

The upshot is that the verdict hardly considered, at least not directly, the potential of the amulets to divert the election's result. The judges were searching for answers in the law, which is supposed to offer the rules for a decent electoral process. The legislature had to have provided guidelines to determine the boundary between fair and unfair influence on the voters. Miraculously, the criterion was found.

The law that permits the use of slogans during elections prohibits the endowment of gifts because the legislators were afraid that gifting might distract the voters' minds: " ... The only means which can be used in election propaganda is the word: the spoken word or the written word. By using words the candidate is allowed to speak to the mind and the logic of the voters in logical items and with convincing reasons. Also he is allowed to captivate by slogans and advertisement tricks ... but the law completely prohibited the use of other means of propaganda. Paragraph 8 of law [659] prohibits the accompaniment of election propaganda with giving presents and other benefits ... using such means, which might disrupt the voter's mind, is unacceptable. The prohibition upon using them, as election propaganda or as part of the propaganda, is total."[24]

As stated previously, in order to make a decision on the legitimacy of the amulets, the judges were looking for references in the law. The result was that the attention was shifted to the question of whether the amulets can be regarded as gifts or not. The judges did not consider the possibility that the potential of these amulets to affect the election results is negligible. They did not examine the option that the potential of the amulets to mislead voters might be marginal compared to other means of propaganda, such as "the spoken word" or "slogans and advertisement tricks." They preferred to interpret the law with regard to the definition of a gift: " ... and inasmuch as the law does not distinguish between a rich and expensive entertainment show and a short voluntary artist performance, and inasmuch as it does not distinguish between serving a large expensive dinner and serving light refreshments, in this manner it does not support any distinction between one gift and another. This means that the prohibition against the endowment of gifts includes not only objects which hold economic value, but also objects without such value."[25]

In short, the dispute in the courtroom was reduced almost to self-parody centering on the burning question of whether the amulet, a miniature bottle of oil, is a forbidden gift or a permissible message like a badge or sticker. One of the highlights of the show was the testimony of the plaintiff's expert witness regarding the testimony of Arie Derei, the political leader of Shas, the party accused in distributing amulets: "... the narrow definition of the member of parliament Arie Derei ... completely ignores the subjective value of the oil bottles to the believers, which might be enormous and great."[26] In other words, the amulets indeed convince those who are already convinced.

To summarize, the judges were searching for answers in the law. Their presupposition was that the law is designed to ensure fair elections. It is the legislators' task to formulate criteria—or, more precisely, general guidelines—to distinguish between fair and unfair influence on the voter. As this case illustrates, however, conclusive criteria may sometimes lead to absurd disputes in the courtroom. The lesson is that human limitations do not exempt even the most august of legislators, and justice, decency, and fairness are only man-made.

NOTES

1. For example, the brave general who carefully prepares the army to defend the west border while the sophisticated enemy plans a surprise attack from the east; the brilliant student who enthusiastically explains his new research to his mediocre, manipulative professor who needs new ideas for his upcoming book; the poor voter who supports the candidate who promise an attractive healthcare program without taking into account that the politician will have to raise taxes substantially to implement the program.

2. The line between manipulative criticism and wild slander is sometimes very thin. Moreover, manipulative slander might give the impression of criticism.

3. Another extreme situation is the case of a politician who is convinced that his blueprint is a verified recipe for failure in the polling booth. He hides his political view and builds his propaganda upon incisive criticism of his opponents. In this way, he crosses the line between decent criticism and manipulative criticism.

4. Compare to Popper, K. R., *The Open Society and Its Enemies* (vol. 2) (London: Routledge, 1996), 162–163: "All political parties have some sort of 'vested interest' in their opponent's unpopular moves. They live by them and are therefore liable to dwell upon, to emphasize, and even to look forward to them. They may even encourage the political mistakes of their opponents as long as they can do so without becoming involved in the responsibility for them. This, together with Engels' theory, has led some

Marxist parties to look forward to the political moves made by their opponents against democracy. Instead of fighting such moves tooth and nails, they were pleased to tell their followers: 'See what these people do. That is what they call democracy. That is what they call freedom and equality! Remember it when the day of reckoning comes.' (An ambiguous phrase which may refer to election day or to the day of revolution). This policy of letting one's opponents expose themselves must, if extended to moves against democracy, lead to disaster. It is a policy of talking big and doing nothing in the face of real and increasing danger to democratic institutions. It is a policy of talking war and acting peace; and it taught the fascists the invaluable method of talking peace and acting war."

5. Compare to Silone, I., *The School for Dictators* (New York and London: Harper & Brothers Publishers, 1938) 45: "The secret of Fascism and National-Socialism must be sought in the first place in the mental state to which the Italian and German masses were reduced as a consequence of the war, the economic crisis, and the failure of the Socialist parties."

6. See, for example, Hayek, F. A., *The Road to Serfdom* (Chicago: University of Chicago Press, 1944) and Silone, I., *The School for Dictators* (New York and London: Harper & Brothers Publishers, 1938).

7. Such cases indicate that a rhetorician who becomes a leader "suddenly" stops convincing.

8. The connection between political economics and choosing the appropriate rules to achieve a beneficial social game has a long scholarly tradition. Adam Smith, the founder of modern economics, perceived political economy as a science that can provide guidelines for choosing rules for the optimal conduct of society (Smith, Adam, *An Inquiry into the Nature and Causes of the Wealth of Nations*, Chicago: University of Chicago Press [1776] 1976). Friedrich Hayek, who has restated the ideas of classical liberalism in the twentieth century, forcefully argued that human beings, limited as we are, have to follow rules in order to better succeed in our personal and social affairs. See for example, Hayek, F. A., *The Constitution of Liberty* (Chicago: University of Chicago Press, 1960), 66: "We all know that, in the pursuit of our individual aims, we are not likely to be successful unless we lay down for ourselves some general rules to which we will adhere without reexamining their justification in every particular instance … The same considerations apply even more where our conduct will directly affect not ourselves but others and where our primary concern, therefore, is to adjust our actions to the actions and expectations of others so that we avoid doing them unnecessary harm." And James Buchanan, the founder of public choice and modern constitutional economics, has argued that the socio-political-economic game must be dependent on an efficient constitution and not on the benevolence of politicians. For a further discussion, see Buchanan, James M., *Choice, Contract and Constitutions*, Vol. 16 of *The Collected Works of James M. Buchanan* (Indianapolis: Liberty Fund, 2001).

9. See Vanberg, V., "Market and State: The Perspective of Constitutional Political Economy," *Journal of Institutional Economics* 1 (1) (2005): 25: "... constitutional economics starts from the recognition that the human agents that populate the world of our experience are imperfect agents, with limited knowledge and limited mental capabilities. Its principal focus is on the working properties of alternative rule regimes or, in Hayek's words, on how the order of rules affects the resulting order of actions. And it is on the practical question of how people can improve the socio-economic-political arrangements within which they live by adopting better 'rules of the game.'"

10. See Vanberg, V., "Market and State," 26: Constitutional economics "as an applied science, as a science that seeks to contribute to the solution of practical social problems, it chooses to concentrate its analytical interest on exploring the issue of how people can jointly improve the constitutional or rule arrangements under which they live, where 'improvement' is strictly defined in terms of what the individuals concerned themselves regard as improvement." Compare also to Hayek (*Rules and Order*, Volume 1 of *Law, Legislation and Liberty* (London: Routledge and Kegan Paul, 1993a), 45): "The question which is of central importance as much for social theory as for social policy is thus what properties the rules must possess so that the separate actions of the individuals will produce an overall order."

11. By paranoia I do not necessarily refer to the common usage—excessive fear of persecution. My focus is more on the clinical sense, as defined by Fried and Agassi (*Paranoia: A Study in Diagnosis*, Dordrecht: D. Reidel Publishing Company, 1976, 2): Paranoia is "an extreme case... of a systematic chronic delusion, logically sustained" or, to put it another way, "... paranoia is by definition a quirk of the intellectual apparatus, a logical delusion."

12. Freud claims that a human being who finds full satisfaction in life never fantasizes (Storr, A., *The Dynamics of Creation*, New York: Ballantine Books, Random House, 1993,20). However, it is very difficult, especially according to Freud, to find such a superman in order to ask him if he ever fantasizes.

13. Such reinforced conception is like Popper's emphasis of the pseudo-scientific components in Freud's and Marx's theories (Fried and Agassi, *Paranoia*, 1976, 44): "... if you accept Freudian theory, all the better; if not, your very resistance, since it expected in the theory, is its confirmation. Likewise, if the capitalist press opposes Marxism, this is as expected; if it on occasion concedes a point to Marxism, that is the result of an inability to resist the force of truth; and if it does neither, it is detracting public attention from the class-struggle—again as expected." I am far from claiming that Popper saw in those theories manipulation for its own sake. Popper tried to show that it is impossible to refute conceptions based upon integrative principles. He cast doubts as to their scientific value. However, it is very hard for any creative human being, including Popper himself, to put aside his human propensity to offer theories immune to criticism.

14. Compare to Walzer, M., *Exodus and Revolution* (New York: Basic Books, 1985).

15. I am repeating and emphasizing throughout this work that, as far as I know, it is impossible to actually read another person's mind, although sometimes we might make a good estimation of his thoughts. The thoughts of Netanyahu and Peres are their own private heritage, and I cannot guarantee that this case reflects manipulative behavior alone (as I am describing). Nevertheless, the historical situation and the documentary material that I read afterward all suggest that intellectual limited manipulation remains a fair categorization of the slogan, "Peres will divide Jerusalem." In spite of my every intention to stick to the exact history, I have to stipulate that my presentation is intended to present a manipulative tactic.

16. The missing component in almost any Palestinian-Israeli substantial peace initiative is public involvement and participation. For a further discussion, see Handelman, S., "Two Complementary Views of Peacemaking: The Palestinian-Israeli Case," in *Middle East Policy* 15 (3) (2008): 57–66.

17. Many additional factors stand in the background. For example, traumatic events in the history of the Jewish people—such as the Holocaust and the painful memory of the destruction of the Temple— passes from one generation to another. My emphasis here is on manipulative techniques. Therefore, the psychological and political background is sketched only in generality and without detailed analysis.

18. Constructing such an elusive message was an intentional strategy of Netanyahu's campaign advisers, such as Arthur Finkelstein: "Arthur read the data, thought a little bit, and said, 'Jerusalem go for it.' The slogan, 'Peres will give up Jerusalem,' was rejected by Arthur. 'Peres will divide Jerusalem' got his confidence. Less technical slogan, said Arthur, less obligated." See Caspit, B., and I. Kafir, *Netanyahu: The Road to Power* (Galey Alpha Communications (in Hebrew), 1997), 272 (my translation).

19. The political structure of Israel, the parliamentary coalition government, necessitates that an efficient and useful campaign has to appeal mainly to the swing voters. This point, as one might expect, was hardly lost on Arthur Finkelstein, Netanyahu's American chief adviser who " ... demanded a large number of surveys, and those were sent to him to U.S.A., including segmentation of swing voters—who they voted for in the past, general political views, occupation, et cetera. The Gallup institute provided the data and Arthur the analysis. 'You are in the picture,' he said to Bibi after he examined the surveys. 'It is possible to win this election.' " See Ibid., 268.

20. As reflected in Keren Neubach's descriptions (*The Race: Elections 96*, Tel-Aviv: Yediot Achronot Press (in Hebrew), 1996, 314.), the potential of the slogan, "Peres will divide Jerusalem," to seize the voters' mind was well known to the members of the Likud, who watched the confrontation between Peres and Netanyahu: " ... Pretty close to beginning of the debate, while Peres committed faith to Jerusalem, a big smile rose on the faces of

the Likudniks. It seemed that this is exactly what they had expected." (my translation).

21. Ironically, precisely during this campaign "it was published...in the inner pages of the news about the de facto division of Jerusalem." Netanyahu's senior campaign adviser, Moti Morel, estimated that Jerusalem was the winning card: "Morel was struggling how to instill in them fighting spirit and searched for a battle slogan. The Golan issue did not look effective to him. Half of the nation is in favor of giving the Golan back. Palestinian state?—Most of the people do not care. Jerusalem? In Jerusalem there is potential." See Caspit B., H. Kristal, and I. Kafir, *The Suicide: A Party Abandons Government* (Tel-Aviv: Avivim Publishing (in Hebrew), 1996) 69 (my translation).

22. For a further discussion on myths and their impact, see Shoham, G. S., *The Dialogue Between the Myth and the Chaos* (Tel-Aviv, Ramot: Tel Aviv University Press, 2002, in Hebrew).

23. See Popper (*The Open Society and Its Enemies*, 23). It is almost inevitable to recall Silone (*The School for Dictators*, 168), who makes fun of fascism and brings the fascist propagandist opinion upon such a sensitive and delicate issue: "The doctrine of suggestion...asserts that suggestion only becomes effective in a state of excitement. Ridicule and fear are both reactions, states of excitement, which favor the intervention of suggestion. Ridicule gives a feeling of superiority, because where there is laughter there is also the prospect of victory. But a strong feeling of fear leads directly to action, because of the sense of danger it gives. Thus ridicule and fear are two components of propaganda which are indispensable for its success. (Hadamowsky, Propoganda und nationale Macht)"

24. Local authority election petition 98/94, "Jerusalem Now" faction headed by Arnon Yekutieli v. Shass, p. 4 (my translation).

25. Ibid. (my translation).

26. Ibid., 3 (my translation).

CHAPTER 8

Spotlight on Leadership: Manipulative Peacemakers

THE ROAD TO HELL IS PAVED WITH GOOD INTENTIONS

Achieving an effective change in human behavior requires employing a certain degree of manipulation.[1] This trivial observation encompasses almost every aspect of social interaction from helping an individual by psycho-therapeutic means to leading society to overcome an essential crisis like a civil war or intractable conflict. Nevertheless, the academic discussion surrounding the use of dubious moral means in order to do "good," at least in the final account, is relatively new.

It is *The Prince*, written by Niccolo Machiavelli 500 years ago, that entered into the academic agenda the connection between immoral means according to reasonably acceptable standards and the greater benefit of society. By introducing a brutal, manipulative gangster as the ultimate redeemer of the Italian society, Machiavelli succeeded in shocking almost every reasonable human being and in shaking up the interminable political-social debate over the conduct of a good society. Machiavelli's outlandishly grotesque proposal, which seemingly contradicts our very basic intuition of ethics and morality, was an innovation at the time it was composed.

Machiavelli's time is well remembered as a period of social crisis. It was a tragic age of endless wars and bloody civil strife, rending Italy into violent regional rivalry. In contrast to the destructive reality, however, the conventional wisdom was that any decent society should be directed according to moral ideals rooted in traditions, such as those of the church and of moral philosophy. The general idea, which sounds simple and attractive, was that a moral, decent society has the potential to diminish evils, wrongs, and destruction. Accordingly, professional politics and statecraft were understood as an ethical mission for well-educated intellectuals who possessed special expertise in ethics and morality.[2] It was a utopian vision of politics, which blocked any possibility of developing a political strategy to lead society to overcome the endless bloody conflicts.

Machiavelli, by writing *The Prince*, turned conventional wisdom on its head.[3] It seems that the author understood very well—sometimes too well—that the road to hell is paved with good intentions. To shake the very foundations of this utopian vision, Machiavelli called a manipulative gangster to the Italian crown. By employing his sophisticated, manipulative cynicism, Machiavelli actually proffered Satan's services toward national salvation.

A MANIPULATIVE REDEEMER FOR SOCIETY IN CRISIS

The Prince is a unique exploration in the mystery of politics. It is an advice book for the common authoritarian leader who has an unlimited appetite for political power. Machiavelli's horrible and shocking recommendations leave a strong impression that politics and morality are concepts and practices that are worlds apart. With his sharp, manipulative cynicism, Machiavelli seems to stretch this point to the very limit.

As strange it may sound, our sophisticated author does not separate statecraft from ethics. Machiavelli has constructed his political agenda on a clear ethical perception. He introduces to his readers a monistic ethical world view, an ethical perception that centers around one specific core value that must be defended almost at any price.[4] The leading value in Machiavelli's thought is the survival of the prince.

According to Machiavelli's distinctive moral perception, any means are qualified to maintain the prince's regime. To put it another way, the ethical value of any political action is measured by its contribution, usefulness, and efficiency to the survival of the prince. The prince himself, Machiavelli's candidate to the Italian crown, is no more than a manipulative gangster.

However, we should not forget the context of Machiavelli's writings: endless civil wars and social strife. To justify his unique perception, Machiavelli offers his readers a simple arithmetic exercise, illustrating that the evils of a dictator who succeeds to stabilize his regime are much smaller relative to the complete destruction of protracted civil wars: "... a prince must not worry about the reproach of cruelty when it is a matter of keeping his subjects united and loyal; for with a very few examples of cruelty he will be more compassionate than those who, out of excessive mercy, permit disorders to continue, from which arise murders and plunderings; for these usually harm the community at large, while the executions that come from the prince harm one individual in particular."[5]

No doubt that we lack good solutions to tragic situations of civil wars, intractable conflicts, and social collapse. Unfortunately, history shows that most conventional methods, techniques, and strategies of peacemaking and conflict resolution did not bring satisfactory results. On the other hand, to propose the service of an authoritarian gangster as the ultimate cure for social crisis smacks of gallows humor or, at least, a dangerous thought of the first modern political scientist who lacks any reasonable social-political theory to offer for such difficult situations. Several questions arise: Are these accusations appropriate? Is Machiavelli's school of statecraft an advanced course in the academy of crime? Is a manipulative criminal able to save a society in crisis?

It is quite acceptable that Machiavelli, by writing an advice book for the common authoritarian leader, had turned the study of politics into an applied science. The dismissed diplomat (that is, Machiavelli) sketches a more realistic picture of politics than the conventional wisdom, which identified efficient statesmanship with ideals like kindness, generosity, and social justice.

However, no person has ever achieved a position of power and leadership by applying Machiavelli's advice.[6] In other words, the thinker who introduces a "special" monistic ethical perception, the survival of the prince at all costs, seems to be a bad adviser or a sinner according to his ethical perception.[7] To understand the logic behind Machiavelli's seemingly grotesque proposal and the lessons it enfolds for society in crisis, we must remember that *The Prince* is only one of Machiavelli's great political treatises.

THE MACHIAVELLIAN SHIFT

Niccolo Machiavelli's most famous political treatises are two compositions that seem to be in direct contradiction: *The Prince* and *The Discourses*.[8] *The Prince* is composed in the manner of a handbook for the common authoritarian leader, while *The Discourse* is an exceptional republican treatise. Ironically, in the dedication of each of these books, Machiavelli claims he is presenting everything he knows. Therefore, one might wonder if Machiavelli, the author whose creations and compositions have been subject of nigh infinite research and unlimited discussions, actually suffered from a split personality. Or is there something more beyond what appears to be such a diametric self-contradiction? Who was the real Machiavelli—a champion of authoritarianism or a passionate advocate of republicanism?[9]

It looks like part of this mystery can be explained in the last chapter of *The Prince*. In this section Machiavelli opens his heart and reveals his prime political dream—the unification of Italy and the restoration of glory to Rome. In this final chapter it becomes clear that in *The Prince* Machiavelli tried to motivate and even manipulate a hungry leader to develop the political power necessary to unite Italy and restore glory to ancient Rome.[10] Accordingly, it is possible to see *The Discourses* as the natural continuation of *The Prince*.

The Prince is stage one—stopping the civil wars and uniting Italy. *The Discourses* is stage two—preventing the new social order from sliding back into chaos by building the foundation for a decent, stable republic.[11] *The Prince* presents a desperate solution to intractable conflict and civil wars, while *The Discourses* provides the recipe to build and preserve a peaceful, stable republic. The glue that connects those two stages is a criminal manipulative leader (*The Prince*) who miraculously transforms himself into a benevolent dictator who wins his place in history forever as the founder of a free and stable republic (*The Discourses*). The leader who begins in infamy ends in virtue. It is of little surprise that a dramatic Machiavellian shift can be found in the biography of the hero of this chapter, Anwar Sadat, the former president of Egypt whose dramatic initiative led to a turning point in the Arab-Israeli conflict.

THE MACHIAVELLIAN TRADITION

The classical republican interpretation of *The Prince*, which I briefly sketched in the last section, may sound very attractive. However, it is not clear at all whether it is true, half true, or completely false. Moreover, it gives Machiavelli a saintly image, when it is not at all clear if he deserves it. In any case, *The Prince* remains notable in the pantheon of social ideas partly because *The Prince* is a signpost in the beginning of a long tradition of scholarship embracing the idea that a post-civil war peaceful social order can emerge only after a strong authoritarian transition period.[12] This tradition, begun with Machiavelli and continued with Hobbes, also encompasses contemporary thinkers, such as Samuel Huntington, and protagonists of the free-market system, such as Friedrich A. Hayek.

Paradoxically, these well-known advocates of personal liberty believe that the only solution to desperate situations of civil wars and intractable conflict is a state builder-dictator. The idea is that the transformation of social chaos to a decent social order can only emerge after a transitional authoritarian period in which the institutional and constitutional foundations for stability are established. In societies that lack the tradition of liberty—such as in cases where the dominant social-political experience is endless violence—it is sometimes necessary to have a "strong leader" to establish the foundations of a good society.

Friedrich Hayek, a passionate advocate of the free-market system as the only feasible alternative to tyranny and fascism, formulated it forcefully: "When a government is in a situation of rupture, and there are no recognized rules ... it is practically inevitable for someone to have almost absolute powers ... It may seem a contradiction that it is I of all people who am saying this, I who plead for limiting government's powers in people's lives and maintain that many of our problems are due, precisely, to too much government. However, when I refer to this dictatorial power, I am talking of a transitional period, solely. As a means of establishing a stable democracy and liberty, clean of impurities. This is the only way I can justify it—and recommend it."[13]

No doubt Machiavelli and Hayek use very appealing rhetoric. In desperate situations it is very attractive to seek the emergence of a strong peacemaking leader. However, the basic questions that the Machiavellian tradition struggles to explain are: How can we guarantee that the strong leader is a benevolent dictator who takes power to complete his historical peacemaking task? How could we be certain that the strong leader is a republican autocrat (Machiavelli), a liberal dictator (Hayek), or a peacemaking tyrant?

Part of the solution to such difficult questions can be found in the pages of *The Prince*. Machiavelli, in his brilliant and shocking rhetoric, offers a simple analysis. An absolute ruler, cruel and manipulative as he might be, will not survive long if he does not act for the benefit of his society (at least in the final account).[14] Acting for the benefit of society means quelling the endless civil wars, uniting Italy, and restoring glory to Rome.

As attractive and brilliant as Machiavelli's insights may seem, we dare never shrink from questioning and wondering: Should we trust a strong ruler to follow Machiavelli's way of thinking? Should we believe that dictators necessarily perceive an overlap between their survival and all crucial altruistic tasks for the benefit of their society, in any final account? Was Machiavelli, 500 years ago, not familiar with vicious dictators like Saddam Hussein, Adolf Hitler, and Benito Mussolini?[15]

MANIPULATING THE MANIPULATOR

Reading *The Prince* with careful attention indicates that this puzzling composition emerges in some twilight zone between imagination and reality. On the one hand, Machiavelli has constructed an imaginary figure of a legendary criminal dictator. On the other hand, it seems that our sophisticated author does not entirely trust "real" human autocrats to understand the pure logic of his super-arch-criminal. There is a gap between Machiavelli's construction of the ideal gangster-ruler and his expectations from real-life human princes to understand and follow Machiavelli's insights on the most efficient statecraft. How does Machiavelli intend to close the gap? How can Machiavelli motivate his unreliable ruler to build the foundation of a good society? Is it possible to persuade a manipulative prince to see an inevitable overlap between his political ambitions and the restoration of order and glory to the Italian society?

In *The Prince*, Machiavelli teaches his ruler all the manipulations, subterfuges, and stratagems that the prince must commit in order to build and stabilize his regime. Machiavelli patiently explains to the prince how to provide the perfect answer at the right time and in the right place. Toward the end of *The Prince*, however, Machiavelli admits that in the long run, achieving and maintaining leadership stability is an impossible mission for any mere mortal. A human prince, as successful and talented as he might be, would not survive politically should he live long enough. Eventually, human limitations, such as entrenched old habits, will prevent the prince from acting and reacting according to the complexity of the ongoing situations, and he will fall from power. The meaning is that the Machiavellian solution to civil war and intractable conflict, a manipulative state builder-dictator, is no more than a cheap illusion founded on a childish psychological desire—the longing for a protective father to solve all of our daunting problems.[16]

However, Machiavelli, the dedicated adviser, does not leave his prince defeated and instead shows him the way to divine glory. Machiavelli promised his unreliable human prince a precious prize—world fame and a place in history forever—but only if he will devote himself to the restoration of order in Italian society: "This opportunity, therefore, must not be permitted to pass by so that Italy, after so long a time, may behold its redeemer. Nor can I express with what love he will be received in all those provinces that have suffered through these foreign floods; with the thirst of revenge, with what obstinate loyalty, with what compassion, with what tears! What doors will be closed to him? Which people will deny his obedience? What jealousy could oppose him? What Italian would deny him homage?"[17] By appealing to the prince's narcissist impulses, Machiavelli attempts to motivate—or more precisely, manipulate—him to undertake great and noble tasks for the benefit of his society.[18]

Unfortunately, most manipulative rulers do not read Machiavelli, Hayek, or any other liberal thinker. As far as history shows, dictators and rulers make their own rules of conduct, at their own whims, and generally their behavior does not follow Machiavelli's logic or his advice. Nevertheless, the sad history of the Arab-Israeli conflict, a painful situation of an intractable conflict, seems to demonstrate many of the insights that Machiavelli proposes in his political writings.

BETWEEN MACHIAVELLIAN PEACEMAKER AND THE ARAB-ISRAELI CONFLICT

The sad history of the Arab-Israeli conflict shows that concrete steps toward peace was finally achieved by the drastic move of a political leader. This leader was not a saint, and his political actions did not necessarily arrive from pure altruism. It was Anwar Sadat, the president of Egypt, whose astonishing visit to Israel in 1977 paved the way to negotiation of a peace agreement between Egypt and Israel.

From a realistic point of view, it appears that Sadat needed to advance a solution to the conflict for his own political survival. Sadat employed a diplomatic offensive in order to offer the Israelis a proposal that they would not be able to reject. Ironically, his dramatic political move enabled the Egyptian dictator to lead the peace process through negotiation and cooperation.

It may be difficult, if not impossible, to fathom the true motivations at work behind the behaviors and activities of human beings.

We cannot see directly into Sadat's mind and soul to explore his way of thinking, but combining the logic of the circumstances (or the complexity of the situation) with insights from Machiavelli's school for statecraft might help us construct a "good" story. And a "good" story, or a fable, whether is true, half true, or completely imaginary, enfolds a lesson. Therefore, I propose to sketch a Machiavellian interpretation to Sadat's historical dramatic move.

Egypt in Sadat's era faced a financial crisis and, as a result, serious social problems. Egypt desperately needed an "economic fuel."[19] Sadat seemed to understand that a peace process with Israel could be extremely valuable for his country in that it could open a window to the west for Egypt and help the country recover the Sinai desert, a beautiful place that attracts tourists from all over the world.

However, it seemed that the Egyptian leader felt trapped because it was clear to him from past painful experiences that it would be extremely difficult to recover the lost asset by force and violence. (Sadat unsuccessfully challenged the very existence of Israel in the 1973 war.) On the other hand, recovering the desert by peaceful means also appeared impossible because the leadership of Israel, which constantly lives in a profound state of concern for Israel's continued existence,[20] was engaged in an uncompromising foreign policy. Israel's policy compelled Sadat to understand that the conventional means of diplomacy and negotiation were doomed to failure.

Any attempt to build bridges between Egypt and Israel was inevitably received with extreme suspicion. Even the most optimistic statesmen were skeptical over the genuine intentions of the two bitter rivals to reach a peace agreement. Therefore, in defiance of any "rational" prediction, the Egyptian leader made an astonishing move. Sadat, the leader of the strongest Arab country and the most rigidly entrenched of Israel's enemies, came to Jerusalem in 1977 to talk peace in the Israeli parliament, the Knesset:

> "I can see the point of all those who were astounded by my decision or those who had any doubts as to the sincerity of the intentions behind the declaration of my decision. No one would have ever conceived that the President of the biggest Arab State, which bears the heaviest burden and the top responsibility pertaining to the cause of war and peace in the Middle East, could declare his readiness to go to the land of the adversary while we were still in a state of war. Rather, we all are still bearing the consequences of four fierce wars waged within thirty years. The families of the

1973 October War are still moaning under the cruel pains of widowhood and bereavement of sons, fathers and brothers. As I have already declared, I have not consulted, as far as this decision is concerned, with any of my colleagues and brothers, the Arab Heads of State or the confrontation States. Those of them who contacted me, following the declaration of this decision, expressed their objection, because the feeling of utter suspicion and absolute lack of confidence between the Arab States and the Palestinian People on the one hand, and Israel on the other, still surges in us all. It is sufficient to say that many months in which peace could have been brought about had been wasted over differences and fruitless discussions on the procedure for the convocation of the Geneva Conference, all showing utter suspicion and absolute lack of confidence."[21]

Not surprisingly, this visit was a turning point in the Arab-Israeli conflict.[22] However, it is not farfetched to consider that this dramatic turning point was part of a bold manipulative strategy—returning the Sinai desert to Egyptian control by a peace agreement with Israel.[23] Therefore, Sadat's historical move seems to rewrite one of the basic rules of *The Prince*: not every subversive manipulation is indecent, at least in the final account: "How praiseworthy it is for a prince to keep his word and to live by integrity and not by deceit everyone knows; nevertheless, one sees from the experience of our times that the princes who have accomplished great deeds are those who have cared little for keeping their promises and who have known how to manipulate the minds of men by shrewdness; and in the end they have surpassed those who laid their foundations upon honesty."[24]

Following the peace agreement, Israel turned over to Egypt the Sinai desert, including oil fields and Israeli air bases. Egypt received from the United States $2 billion in tanks, planes, and artifact weaponry, in addition to foreign aid allocation of $1 billion.[25] Unfortunately, the relationship between Egypt and Israel has never evolved beyond a cold peace. These results indicate that, after all, Machiavelli's manipulative methods of peacemaking, negotiation, and reconciliation look like the persistence of war by peaceful means.[26]

If there is any truth in my interpretation of Sadat's way of thinking, then it is worth recalling Machiavelli's brilliant insight into how the personal ambition of a "hungry" leader might operate for the benefit of society.[27] In Sadat's case, Egypt acquired Sinai, and both countries gained peace. As attractive and heroic as our short story of manipulative initiative might sound, however, the final results are not as glorious as they are in fairy tales because any drastic political move is likely to have unintended and unpredictable implications.

One of the immediate results of the peace process between Egypt and Israel was that no Arab state would attempt war with Israel. This achievement has contributed to the Palestinization of the Arab-Israeli conflict[28] and to the breaking of Gamal Abdel Nasser's (Sadat's predecessor) utopian dream of Pan-Arabism, two tendencies that actually started after the Six Day War. On the other hand, Sadat's initiative added to the vacuum in the Arab world, which was created after the failure of the Pan-Arabism aspirations, and gave a push to the rise of political Islam. Unfortunately, Sadat paid a dear price for his peace initiative. On October 6, 1981, radical Islamists assassinated him.

NOTES

1. See Kelman, H. C., "Manipulation of Human Behavior: An Ethical Dilemma for the Social Scientist," in *Journal of Social Issues* 21, no. 2 (1965): 33.

2. Ironically, Machiavelli, who proved excellence in humanist studies, was chosen to serve as a diplomat at the age of 29. See Skinner, Q., *Machiavelli* (Oxford: Oxford University Press, 1981), 3–4.

3. For a further discussion on the Machiavellian revolution in modern political philosophy, see Mannet, P., *An Intellectual History of Liberalism*, R. Balinski (trans.) (Princeton: Princeton University Press, 1996), 10–19, and Strauss, L., *An Introduction to Political Philosophy* (Detroit: Wayne State University Press, 1989), 39–51.

4. In contrast to monistic ethical-political theories that center on one core super-value, pluralism is usually associated with the idea that there are irreducibly many prudential values. For a further discussion on the monism-pluralism issue, see Griffin, J., *Well-Being: Its Meaning, Measurement and Moral Importance* (Oxford: Clarendon Press, 1986), 89–92.

5. See Machiavelli, N., *The Prince* in P. Bondanella and M. Musa (Eds.) *The Portable Machiavelli* (New York: Penguin Books, 1979), 130. There are many interpretations of *The Prince*, indicating that Machiavelli saw the authoritarian regime as a desperate alternative to the devastating and nigh total chaos that was so common in his time. For a further discussion, see Dietz, M. G., "Trapping The Prince: Machiavelli and the Politics of Deception," in *The American Political Science Review*, 80 (1986): 778–779.

6. Compare to Silone, I., *The School for Dictators* (New York and London: Harper & Brothers Publishers, 1938), 26.

7. The very inapplicability of Machiavelli's advice to realistic application was the basis for many interpretations of *The Prince*. For example, Dietz

("Trapping The Prince," 777–799) noted that the intentions of Machiavelli, who was outcast by the Medici, were actually to trap the prince. According to this interpretation, Machiavelli hoped that Lorenzo de Medici, to whom he dedicated *The Prince*, would follow his deliberately poisonous bad advice and that it would lead him to eventually lose his regime.

8. See Machiavelli, *The Prince* and Machiavelli, N., *The Discourses* in P. Bondanella and M. Musa (Eds.) *The Portable Machiavelli* (New York: Penguin Books, 1979a).

9. For a different formulation of this question, see Mansfield, H., "Necessity in the Beginnings of Cities" in A. Parel (ed.) *The Political Calculus* (Toronto and Buffalo: University of Toronto Press, 1972), 102.

10. See Strauss, *An Introduction to Political Philosophy*, 44–47, and Agassi, J., *Technology: Philosophical and Social Aspects* (Dordrecht, Holland: D. Reidel Publishing Company, 1985), 193.

11. Compare to Dietz ("Trapping The Prince," 780).

12. See, for example, Wantchekon, L., "The Paradox of 'Warlord' Democracy: A Theoretical Investigation," in *American Political Science Review* Vol. 98 (1) (2004): 17–32.

13. Hayek F. A., interviews in El Mercurio (Santiago, Chile, 1981) from http://www.hayekcenter.org/takinghayekseriouslyarchive/005571.html.

14. This point arises many times in Machiavelli's text. See, for example, Machiavelli (*The Prince*, 153).

15. Compare to Femia, who claims that "the ideology of Italian fascism is permeated by Machiavellian themes and principles." Femia J., "Machiavelli and Italian Fascism," *History of Political Thought* 25 (1) (2004): 1–15.,

16. Compare to Freud's (1968) opinion—or more precisely, diagnosis—of the religion phenomenon. Freud, Sigmund, "The Future of an Illusion," in *The Standard Edition of the Complete Psychological Works of Sigmund Freud* 21: 3–56, Translated by James Strachey (London: Hogarth Press, 1968).

17. See Machiavelli (*The Prince*, 165–166).

18. Compare to Strauss (*An Introduction to Political Philosophy*, 42): "The passion in question is the desire for glory. The highest form of the desire for glory is the desire to be a new prince in the fullest sense of the term, a wholly new prince: a discoverer of a new type of social order, a molder of many generations of men. The founder of society has a selfish interest in the preservation of society, of his work. He has therefore a selfish interest in the members of his society being and remaining sociable, and hence good."

19. See, for example, Hirst, D., and I. Beeson, *Sadat* (London: Farber and Farber, 1981), 252–254.

20. It appears that the fear and worry which are fundamental to the Jewish-Israeli essence were well known to the Egyptian president. In his historical speech in the Israeli parliament, Sadat had repeated several times that every peace agreement will have to include guarantees to ensure security for Israel: "What is peace for Israel? It means that Israel lives in the region with

her Arab neighbors, in security and safety. To such logic, I say yes. It means that Israel lives within her borders, secure against any aggression. To such logic, I say yes. It means that Israel obtains all kinds of guarantees that ensure those two factors. To this demand, I say yes. More than that: we declare that we accept all the international guarantees you envisage and accept." Sadat, A., "Statement to the Knesset by President Sadat," in Special Meeting of the Knesset: the Forty-Third Meeting of the Ninth Knesset (November 20, 1977), Jerusalem.

21. Sadat's speech at the Israeli parliament on November 20, 1977 ("Statement to the Knesset by President Sadat").

22. For a further discussion on Sadat's trip to Jerusalem as a major turning point in the Arab-Israeli conflict, see Kelman, H. C., "Overcoming the Psychological Barrier: An Analysis of the Egyptian-Israeli Peace Process," *Negotiation Journal* 1, (3) (1985): 213–234.

23. In this context, it seems important to pay attention that Sadat's historical speech in the Israeli parliament is not clean from demagogic motifs. For example, he approaches the Israeli Jews and says: "You have to give up ... the belief that force is the best method for dealing with the Arabs." Of course, such preaching does not come from a liberal ruler that respects the democratic rights of his people.

24. See Machiavelli (*The Prince*, 133).

25. See Bickerton, I. J., and C. L. Klausner, *A Concise History of the Arab Israeli Conflict* 5th ed. (Englewood Cliffs, NJ: Prentice Hall, 2007), 190–191.

26. Compare to famous controversial quotation by Carl von Clausewitz, the well-known philosopher of war: "War is not a mere act of policy but a true political instrument, a continuation of political activity by other means." Or the Sun Tzu's famous maxim: "All is War."

27. About two hundred years later, Adam Smith formulated a basic principle in modern economics: "It is not from the benevolence of the butcher, the brewer, or the baker, that we expect our dinner, but from their regard to their own interest. We address ourselves, not to their humanity, but to their self-love, and never talk to them of our necessities but of their advantages." In a similar vein to Machiavelli, Smith points out that it is better to count on the self interest of human beings than to expect altruistic initiatives. Smith, A., *An Inquiry into the Nature and Causes of the Wealth of Nations* (Chicago: University of Chicago Press, [1776] 1976).

28. Compare to Kelman, H. C., "The Palestinianization of the Arab-Israeli Conflict," *The Jerusalem Quarterly* 46 (1988): 3–15.

CHAPTER 9
Introducing Manipulations That Open Our Minds

INTRODUCTION

"Expanding manipulations," or manipulations that open minds, steer the target's mind to consider additional options. The tendency is to enable the target, entrenched in old habits or erroneous fixations, to take a wider world view, but without the manipulator directly intervening in his final decision. I present two manipulative strategies, emotional and intellectual, to achieve the desired effect. The emotional strategy maneuvers the target to examine his world view from different perspectives by playing on his most intimate emotions. The intellectual strategy maneuvers the target to doubt his world view by employing a dramatic and even shocking move. Let us explore, examine, and understand the logic, motivations, and difficulties behind these unusual manipulative strategies.

BETWEEN FIXATION AND MANIPULATION

I have demonstrated that manipulating people to adopt a biased world perception can be an effective motivating strategy, as it affects the target's judgment of reality and maneuvers him to take the manipulator's goal as first priority. Unfortunately, people are often fervently delusional enough on their own. The individual "possessed" by conviction is entirely unwilling to engage in any critical discussion regarding his beliefs, behavior, and actions, even when he asks for help.

Conviction in a closed, biased world view is a well-known phenomenon in almost every walk of life. Let me demonstrate this tragic phenomenon and its disastrous implications in three important areas: military, psychotherapy, and science. Research indicates that many strategic surprises in wars succeeded because of the sheer closedmindedness of military leaders. Generals who were so possessed by a biased, closed conviction confused real, false, relevant, and irrelevant information. They veritably turned reality on its head. They interpreted almost any reliable and credible information that contradicted their mistaken view as false and, vice versa, any false information that supported their mistaken conception as naked truth. For example, Israel was almost exterminated in the 1973 war, which began with a surprise attack. There was a broad consensus among Israeli military and political leaders that the enemy would not attack. The Egyptians and the Syrians took the opportunity to surprise the Israeli army, which was not prepared for a war.[1]

Observations in the field of psychology show that often enough there is a gap between the source of suffering (the "real" reason) and the rational explanation that the psychological patient gives to his misery (the "good" reason). Constructing a logical but mistaken paradigm (the "good" reason) is often called rationalization. Rationalization is a defense mechanism that helps people view unbearable reality in a better light by employing rational justifications. (For example, a parent may claim that his son fails at school because the teachers cannot appreciate the student's unique talents.) In the more extreme cases, the patient who cries for help is not willing to cast doubts on his rational conception, which plays a key role in his suffering. He continues to employ every good reason and rational argument to support his biased explanation. (As far as I know, this phenomenon is labeled as insanity.)[2]

Thomas Kuhn, the famous historian of science, was fully aware of the phenomenon of closed, biased conviction in the progressive world of science. He reminded us that science changes because old scientists die.[3] Sir Francis Bacon, the great thinker, showed hysterical hostility toward the idea of inventing scientific theories on the metaphorical drawing board. Bacon was afraid that the scientist would refuse to consider the possibility that his theory might be false, even when the evidence lay before his very eyes. Indeed, there are many jokes about the crazy scientist enamored with a pet theory even when its falsification is quite obvious.[4]

Conviction in a mistaken conception is a multidimensional phenomenon. For example, it has social aspects, cultural components, and psychological factors. Of course, fixation is not without cost. Often enough, the closed-minded individual pays a heavy personal price for his stubbornness and inflexibility. On the other hand, it is reasonable to assume that he finds certain functionality, and even survival functionality, in holding to a problematic conception (otherwise he would not so obsessively refuse to examine it critically). For example, it is more pleasant for us to believe that our suffering results from too much importance than from impotence (similarly to the miserable paranoid, who is persecuted by the dark forces because he has to save the world). It is sometimes easier for a proud young man to blame his family in the failure of his relationship than to simply admit that the love of his life has someone else in mind.

The crucial point is that a closed-minded person not only refuses to give up his paradigm, but also goes to every effort to prevent any critical discussion that seems to be relevant to the subject. He is not listening to the facts, nor to others, and not even to certain aspects of himself. Unfortunately, the more pathological cases, such as the clinical paranoid, seem helpless. We do not have a cure for chronic delusional disorders like the disease Paranoia Vera.[5] However, in the more "normal" instances, the hope to achieve an effective change might be found in an unusual action. The default alternative seems to be a sophisticated manipulative strategy. (Of course, the option to leave the fixated individual alone, as long has he does not hurt someone else, always remains.)[6]

THE "LIBERAL" MANIPULATOR

Almost every manipulation interferes in the decision making of a person without his approval. Even the most benevolent manipulator, who has the best intentions, employs questionable moral means, such as misdirection, trickery, and leading astray, to influence the target. The practical meaning is that manipulation's intentions to maneuver the target for his own benefit seem somewhat paternalistic.

Paternalism means to act for the benefit of another person without getting his approval.[7] The paternalist acts like a father who treats his fellow like a little child. Paternalism is considered distinctly inconsistent with the liberal tradition, which has always emphasized the importance of liberty, independence, and free choice. Expanding manipulations are intended to provide the opportunity to manipulate the target for his benefit without contradicting liberal values.

In contrast with limiting manipulations that aim to limit the target's field of vision, expanding manipulations are designed to enable the target to consider a wider range of possible options before making a decision. To be more specific, expanding manipulations maneuver the target to examine his decisions and problems from different perspectives and with respect to any final choice that the target is going to make.

The liberal philosophy, in general, praises the expansion of options and condemns limitations. Our "liberal manipulator" identifies an improvement in his target's condition with an expanded field of vision. Moreover, a liberal manipulator operates under the assumption that a successful expanding manipulation will lead the target to choose the best option according to the target's preferences, priorities, and best interests. Indeed, this is a significant liberal characteristic. On the other hand, the "benevolent manipulator" believes that there is a strong resistance in the target's mind to consider additional options. The meaning is that expanding manipulations, after all, encompass paternalistic elements. The different, or even contrasting, tendencies of paternalism versus liberalism suggest that expanding manipulation appears a strange admixture that can be labeled as "liberal paternalism."[8] The question is: Could manipulation ever rightly be considered paternalistic?

Often enough it appears that the target is speaking in two voices. On the one hand, he may ask for help and even pay good money to get it, such as seeing a therapist. On the other hand, he consistently operates against his own benefit and best interests. For example, he may enter psychoanalysis but refuse to discuss his most intimate secrets that cause him a great deal of suffering; he may strictly take diabetic medicines but continue to smoke and eat sugary food; he may wish to get over his ex-wife but continue to keep the bond alive through unproductive litigation. To which voice of the target should the liberal manipulator listen, the one that is crying for help or to the other that objects to any practical option for change?

The term liberal paternalism might sound all the more jarring for a more general reason. Usually, paternalism is related to the physical sphere in that one person is acting, physically, for the benefit of another one without getting his permission. In contrast, the manipulations that are discussed within the scope of this book operate mainly in the mental dimension. Therefore, speaking about paternalism in the context of manipulation might sound strange and inappropriate. The next example will demonstrate the difficulty.

Classical liberals support the right to commit suicide and object to almost any attempts to physically prevent a person from killing himself. However, even the most radical liberals are not against arguing with, convincing, and even manipulating a person in order to change his mind about committing suicide. Therefore, coining the term liberal paternalism, especially in the context of expanding manipulations, might be an unnecessary semantic complication.

The examples in the next chapter demonstrate that a theoretical debate on the meaning, or perhaps nonmeaning, of the term liberal paternalism might run into serious practical problems. To be more specific, trying to manipulate the target's mind for his best interests is not an easy task even for the most capable manipulator, and such a move might lead to unexpected results.

EXPANDING OR LIMITING CHOICES

Our point of departure is a liberal manipulator who believes that his target is a closed-minded and biased individual. The benevolent manipulator understands that the target's problematic position is somewhat functional for him, the target. For example, the target prefers to escape into a sweet imaginary fantasy than to cope with extremely difficult circumstances. Our liberal manipulator decides to help, or maybe to save, the target. However, it is reasonable to expect that the target will not stay apathetic to any move intended to shift his "precious" conception, so the liberal manipulator's road to open new horizons for the target is fraught with obstacles. Could it be that the difficult circumstances will eventually turn a liberal manipulator into a paternalistic or even oppressive one? Is it possible that our liberal manipulator, who has his own opinion, is actually leading the target to embrace the manipulator's position? Will it be too much of exaggeration to wonder if expanding manipulations are, in practice, no more than theoretical camouflage for limiting manipulations?

These questions are not new and certainly not original. For example, generations of psychologists have been tortured, and still are, by the very question of the neutrality of the psychological therapy. There are strong arguments that any therapist, like every one of us, can never be neutral, as he has his own opinion of the patient's situation.[9] The neutral, or maybe the liberal, expectations of the therapist—"only" to help the patient to discover new options, possibilities and horizons—are not realistic. Is it possible that the therapist, in practice, is leading his patient to embrace one specific position that is, incidentally, his own? Is it possible that the therapist who starts his job with liberal intentions becomes a paternalistic therapist in the better case and an authoritarian therapist in the worst one?

These difficulties are highly relevant to many other areas in the social sciences, among them the difference between a liberal education and an oppressive one; the boundary between constructive criticism and destructive criticism; and the distinction between social reformer, social spoiler, and social oppressor. However, it is the psychological treatment that provides laboratory conditions to examine these difficult problems. The next chapters examine the interrelationships of ethical difficulties in therapeutic sessions and general problems in the wider social context. This methodology should help pave the way to understanding the complicated interaction between a liberal manipulator and his target.

NOTES

1. For a further discussion on strategic surprises in wars, see, for example, Wohlstetter R., *Pearl Harbor: Warning and Decision* (Stanford, CA: Stanford University Press, 1962) and Whaley, B., *Codeword Barbarossa* (Cambridge: The MIT Press, 1974). Of course, they dig much deeper than the schematic and brief description that I offer here. My purpose is only to demonstrate the strength of conviction in a conception that contradicts the facts on the ground.

2. For a further discussion on rationalization, see Grunbaum, A., *The Foundations of Psychoanalysis: A Philosophical Critique* (London: University of California Press, 1985), 70; Szabadoa, B., "The Self, Its Passions and Self Deception," in M. Mike (Ed.) *Self-Deception, and Self-Understanding* (KS: University Press of Kansas, 1985), 155.

3. See Kuhn, T. S. *The Structure of Scientific Revolutions* (Chicago: Chicago University Press, 1962).

4. See, for example, Fried, Y., and J. Agassi, *Paranoia: A Study in Diagnosis* (Dordrecht: D. Reidel Publishing Company, 1976), 31: " ... Bacon's bad scientist, who instead of waiting for the facts to lead him to a theory, dares to invent one and test it empirically. Clearly, said Bacon, his test will not be of any use since he will not give up his theory just because a small fact contradicts it. This, added Bacon, is especially true if he has disciples. He will have a fixation on it; he will rather distort ad hoc, either his theory or his facts, than give up his pet doctrine and the advantage it gives him over his disciples. And, unable to take the cure of accepting facts which run contrary to his

theory, he will be trapped in his error; his theory, thus, will act as both spectacles and blinkers."

5. See Fried and Agassi, *Paranoia*.

6. Compare to Berlin, I., *Four Essays on Liberty* (Oxford: Oxford University Press, 1975), 21–23: "It is this change of attitude to the function and value of the intellect that is perhaps the best indication of the great gap which divided the twentieth century from the nineteenth ... For the first time it was now conceived that the most effective way of dealing with questions, particularly those recurrent issues which had perplexed and often tormented original and honest minds in every generation, was not by employing the tools of reason, still less those of the more mysterious capacities called 'insight' and 'intuition,' but by obliterating the questions themselves. And this method consists not in removing them by rational means—by proving, for example, that they are founded on intellectual error or verbal muddles or ignorance of the facts—for to prove this would in its turn presuppose the need for rational methods of philosophical or psychological argument. Rather, it consists in so treating the questioner that problems which appeared at once overwhelmingly important and utterly insoluble vanish from the questioner's consciousness like evil dreams and trouble him no more. It consists, not in developing the logical implications and elucidating the meaning, the context, or the relevance and origin of a specific problem—in seeing what it amounts to—but in altering the outlook which gave rise to it in the first place." It seems that Berlin's description is too much of an exaggeration. As I will try to demonstrate, change, even by employing creative and unusual approaches, is not easy.

7. See, for example, Suber, P., "Paternalism," in C. B. Gray (Ed.) *Philosophy of Law: An Encyclopedia* (New York: Garland Publishing, 1999): "Paternalism" comes from the Latin pater, meaning to act like a father, or to treat another person like a child ... In modern philosophy and jurisprudence, it is to act for the good of another person without that person's consent, as parents do for children. It is controversial because its end is benevolent, and its means coercive. Paternalists advance people's interests (such as life, health, or safety) at the expense of their liberty."

8. To better clarify the term liberal paternalism I would like to explain its difference from somewhat similar notion, libertarian paternalism. Thaler and Sunstein (Thaler, R. H., and C. R. Sunstein, "Libertarian Paternalism," *The American Economic Review* 93(2) (2003): 175–179), who appear to have coined the term libertarian paternalism, view it "as an approach that *preserves freedom of choice* but that authorizes both private and public institutions *to steer people in directions that will promote their welfare*." (the emphasis is mine). Liberal paternalism, however, is a motivating strategy geared toward expanding people's field of vision on existing options. In contrast to the libertarian paternalist, who seems to know, or at least estimate, that a specific option is likely to promote another's welfare, the liberal paternalist identifies a larger

spectrum of possibilities with improving people's well being. Thaler and Sunstein seem to emphasize the paternalistic aspect of their unusual mixture libertarian paternalism, while in my own somewhat strange coupling, liberal paternalism, the emphasis remains the liberal aspect.

9. The twentieth century taught us to sober up from the illusion of possible neutrality and objectivity. Even Freud, who claimed that psychoanalysis is an objective science, was far from being detached or neutral. For a further discussion, see Szasz, T. S., *The Myth of Mental Illness* (New York: Harper & Row, 1974), 257.

CHAPTER 10

Spotlight on Therapy: Therapeutic Manipulation

THE POWERFUL SUPERVISOR AND HIS ATTRACTIVE SECRETARY

Many stories have been written about the "winning team" of the beautiful, ambitious secretary and her demanding supervisor. Of course, ordinary people are not often as fascinating and glamorous as those presented in Hollywood movies. However, some of the ethical dilemmas that even grade-B movies present, in order to evoke audience sympathy, do actually have some basis in ordinary workday reality. Indeed, it is not difficult to dramatize such a meeting between a secretary and her superior, and thus to present an important real-life ambiguity: the difference between legitimate courtship and sexual harassment.

In order to dramatize the issue, let us assume that both characters have ulterior motives. The ambitious secretary schemes for a promotion at any cost, while her womanizing superior lusts after her. Therefore, they are both involved in a contest that creates almost impossible difficulties for an impartial spectator wanting to identify the "real" manipulator: Is it the beautiful, elegant, wily, and ambitious secretary or is it her powerful and domineering, but lonely and frustrated superior?

This dilemma becomes extremely difficult in cases where our dramatis personae, the superior and his secretary, have many desirable career options opening up to them, are working together completely of their own volition, and are able to resign whenever they want. Since each of them has sufficient self-determination to fulfill his or her dreams and desires, the interaction becomes a mutually manipulative game; that is, until the situation escalates out of control. Unfortunately, the interaction that starts as a mutual manipulative diversion often ends in reciprocal accusation and litigation. For example, the disappointed secretary, who did not get the promotion, accuses her superior—or, more precisely, her former superior—of sexual harassment. He, frustrated at her rejection and scorn, responds by claiming deception and entrapment in her provocative behavior and use of feminine wiles.

As is well known, many human interactions create tensions and confrontations. The most important question is not how to resolve such an archetypical conflict, but how to avoid it. Indeed, the more productive riddle is whether it is possible to channel the opposing motivations of the secretary and her superior to create a real winning team, a team that works together in harmony and yields beneficial results. My intention is not to confront this challenging ethical issue in a real-life workplace. Rather, my chief purpose is to shed light on a similar ambiguity that appears in a more discrete situation, the psychological treatment. Accordingly, I move from manipulative courting in the workplace and delve into the dark corners of a human relationship as it appears in the laboratory conditions of a therapist's couch.

Speaking of courtship and therapeutic interaction, it is common that when two human beings meet, even occasionally, to discuss the most intimate secrets of one of them, they will probably not remain indifferent to each other. Moreover, it was Freud, the founder of psychoanalysis, who interpreted these meetings as being most relevant to the ambiguous connection between manipulation and legitimate courtship. Freud explained most of human misery psychosexually. Likewise was his view of psychoanalysis itself, with its emphasis on the well-known phenomenon of transference-love that is an essential component in Freudian therapy and is relevant to the discussion of manipulative behavior and sexual courtship. But let us begin with some general background.

THE FREUDIAN COUCH AND MANIPULATION

A person usually comes to psychoanalysis because of distress that she[1] cannot cope with by herself. Unfortunately, it turns out that getting to the root of psychological problems is not easy. Often, the patient actually seems to conceal key issues that have crucial bearing upon her misery. In order to elicit honest expression and gain access to the source of her hurt, the therapist must offer compelling incentives both to distract the patient's mind from her usual defenses and to motivate her to act in unpleasant manners, such as when revealing her most intimate secrets. Examples of such powerful motivating incentives are love and sexual desire.

Love and sexual desire work a powerful magic that can blind even the most reasonable human being. However, the inevitable questions arise: What is the connection between such incentives and psychoanalysis? More precisely, how exactly must the analyst employ such powerful tools for the benefit of the patient? Why not employ as interrogators top models in order to ease the patients of their secret burdens? Or, maybe a necessary prerequisite for becoming an analyst is a natural talent for seduction?

One need not be Freud to realize that choosing sex and love as the motivating mechanisms in psychoanalysis raises significant ethical problems. Moreover, analysts, including Freud himself, do not always look like movie stars. Nevertheless, as I will explain later, love and sex are often viewed as motivating vehicles of psychoanalytic sessions, at least in Freud's way of thinking. Before plunging into the controversy over eroticism in psychoanalysis, however, we continue with more necessary general background.

THE MANIPULATOR THAT MIGHT FALL VICTIM OF HIS OWN TRAP

The idea of "therapeutic" manipulation is based on the observation that the typical psychoanalytic client will not readily facilitate the analyst's work, which is to help the patient make a change. With this in mind, Freud saw in the transference-love phenomenon—the erotic feelings of a meaningful childhood image (usually a mother or father) that the patient projects onto the analyst—as an opportunity to lead the patient to examine major aspects of his or her life from a new perspective. To be more specific, Freud hoped to use the erotic feelings that psychoanalysis provokes to maneuver the patient into discovering details from her early life that are relevant to her present suffering.

Ironically, it seems that Freud, occupied in developing his paradigm, did not explore the possibility that he, himself, might be the victim of manipulation. In other words, being occupied in devising a manipulative method for the patient's benefit, it seems to have evaded

Freud's thinking that it might be the patient who was maneuvering the analysis.[2]

The idea of such modification in classical Freudian psychoanalysis is implicit in the thought of Thomas Szasz, one of the sharpest critics of Freud. According to Szasz's way of thinking, transference-love is the childish behavior of a patient who searches for a protective father or a fairy godmother. To put it differently, by imitating infantile patterns, the patient hopes to maneuver the analyst into taking responsibility for the patient's behavior and decision-making.

My central claim in this chapter is that there is truth in the extreme views of Freud and Szasz; both the analyst and the patient strive to manipulate. Accordingly, I propose the possibility that the seemingly contradictory views of Freud and Szasz are actually complementary. In order to demonstrate this idea, this chapter stages an imaginary scenario—a meeting between a classical Freudian analyst and a figure of my own construction, inspired by Thomas Szasz's critique of psychoanalysis, of a typical Szaszian patient. This model will, I hope, delineate the scope of the controversial discussion over the transference-love phenomenon and lead the way to new ideas in psychoanalysis.

"MENTAL ILLNESS" AND MANIPULATION

In times of extreme distress there is a tendency toward escapism. Instead of coping with their real problems, people commonly fantasize about a much "friendlier" world and often of some protective father figure to rescue them.[3] Freud believed that all life involves continual distress that people find difficult to cope with. Therefore, in every one of us is hidden a child that sometimes maneuvers our behavior in ways not always beneficial. Indeed, searching for a protective father was one of Freud's classical explanations for such social phenomena as religion.[4] Are those childish patterns of behavior simply innate to our nature?

It is almost beyond controversy that childhood, especially at an early stage, has an important influence on our mature life, and it is well known that adults tend to repeat childish patterns whenever they face difficulties. Of course, everyone has his unique character, weaknesses, and frustrations. Infantile patterns or, in professional language, symptoms, vary from one person to the next. For example, in times of pressure one person will start fantasizing and another will begin stuttering.

Freud thought the source of such problems is hidden in an early stage of development. For example, a traumatic event may prevent a child from developing normal skills for coping with a frustrating reality. As a result, some childish patterns are embraced and continue to be used in adult life.[5] In other words, the traumatic event has cut deeply into the patient's psyche, remaining unhealed. In order to recover, according to Freud, a patient needs "mental surgery."[6] This "mental surgery" is not a simple one because the scar—or, more precisely, the open wound—is shielded by defenses. As the person grows older and experiences more frustrations, the defenses harden. In order to bypass defensive obstacles and heal the wound, manipulative behavior is required.

This last description of the psychological therapeutic procedure might give the impression that "mental doctors" have expertise in "surgery" of the psyche. In other words, it may seem that "mental doctors" are well trained in the medical operation of their patients' psyche, using conversation and manipulative behaviors. The source of this possible confusion is that it is not always clear whether such images as "mental surgery" and "bleeding scar" are metaphors or "real" medical terminology. This is exactly one of the main points of Thomas Szasz's critique.[7]

According to Szasz, illness is a physical state of the body. To be more specific, it describes the body as a broken machine. Just as insufficient water in the radiator will cause the engine of an automobile to overheat, the flu will weaken the human immune system and often cause fever. Accordingly, medical terms such as mental illness, which describe the health of our psyche, should be regarded as metaphors and not be interpreted literally. Szasz points out that mental illness is a metaphor from the material world (illness viewed as a broken machine), borrowed to describe a mental state. Unfortunately, many people, especially mental doctors like Freud, tend to forget that mental illness is only a metaphor and come to regard it far too literally— "the soul is sick."

Taking the term mental illness as literally true leads to a phenomenon labeled psychiatric imperialism. It began with labeling the neurotic as sick. Next came the pretender or, in medical terms, the malingerer, so labeled because his mental condition seemed to be much more severe because its cause seemed to be buried much deeper in his psyche.[8] Of course, the inevitable end to this mode of labeling is that we are all crazy and need some kind of "mental surgery."[9] The irony of fate, however, is that no one, including mental doctors, is endowed with an X-ray enabling him to test the "medical" condition of one's psyche.

According to Szasz, mental illness is actually no more than the manipulative behavior of the weak in society in a desperate attempt to attract attention; it is a hopeless strategy of crying out for help.[10] Ironically and sadly, the confusing medical terminology, such as mental patient, mental hospitals, and mental surgery, does not benefit the patient. On the one hand, it may deprive him of his freedom against his will, as when he is hospitalized in a mental hospital.[11] On the other hand, it may encourage him not to take responsibility for his own life. It may be especially damaging to people who seek attention by displaying childish behavior because their sense of responsibility is so low to begin with.

Szasz generally agrees with Freud that our childhood is a critical time in our development. In contrast to Freud, however, Szasz views "acting like a baby" more as a habit that the patient, reaching out for help, has to learn to overcome. Therefore, Szaszian therapy, in contrast to Freudian therapy, is more like learning to cope with reality and its many problems than it is a search for the early development of symptoms and behavior inappropriately carried over into adult life.

Both Freud and Szasz recognize the importance of knowledge for increasing the patient's quality of life. However, their emphases are different. Freud asserts that the patient's recovery depends on discovering painful details from her biography that lie hidden deep in her unconscious, whereas Szasz recommends that therapy should focus on the practical knowledge that the patient needs to acquire in order to improve her ability to cope with everyday life.[12] Therefore, according to Freud, the therapeutic office functions like an "operating room" for the soul, whereas Szaszian psychological interaction more resembles a joint study in a liberal classroom.[13] One central point of this essential dispute is their different opinions regarding the transference-love phenomenon.

TRANSFERENCE-LOVE AS A "THERAPEUTIC" MANIPULATION

The analyst's main task, at least according to Freud, is relieving the patient's misery.[14] However, a major part of the suffering is caused by the existence of an immense gap between the patient's "true" preferences and her conscious knowledge thereof. Therefore, the patient first has to become aware of her own true desires and, second, to decide on some tenable course of action. However, there is an internal barrier that disconnects the patient from consciousness of desires and strategic necessities to fulfillment. In order to enable the patient to break through and reconnect to her deepest self, a manipulative strategy must be employed.

One convincing method concretizing this "therapeutic" strategy is the motivating mechanism in the analytical session: transference-love. By using the patient's most intimate feelings, Freud hoped to successfully maneuver her to discover painful, deeply repressed details from her early life. In this unusual manner, Freud hoped to "open" for her the possibility to examine her course of life from a different and more fruitful perspective. Thus, the analyst performs the role of the rescuer, as Prince Charming releasing the patient from her suffering by gaining access to her frustrated sexual desire.

Transference-love, according to Freud, is not ordinary love. It is a particular love in the sense that the patient does not actually fall in love with the analyst, although that, too, is possible.[15] According to Freud, the patient projects her own fantasies onto the analyst. The patient recasts the analyst in the light of a meaningful character from her early childhood (usually a mother or father) along with forbidden longings (more precisely, sexual desire) towards him. During the analytic interaction, the forgotten sexual desires from early childhood reemerge in the patient's mind, but in a way that makes her unable to distinguish between the analyst and the sexual object of her early childhood.[16] The question arises: What is the therapeutic value of such a phenomenon?

The transference paradigm is built on the assumption that the "abstract" child, hidden in the patient's mind and making her life so miserable, was once concrete. Unfortunately, the concrete child had to contend with a difficult situation. She felt strong sexual desire for a dominant character in her childhood that could not be fulfilled. The trouble was that the child "refused" to give up that unrealistic desire. This contradiction (the unwillingness to concede and inability to fulfill) led to a distorted compromise: repression. Repression occurs when compelling wishes sink deep into the patient's unconscious. The practical implication is that those wishes operate under the supervision of a selective guard. On the one hand, the faithful guard enables the childish wishes to maneuver the patient to operate subversively to her declared aspirations. On the other hand, the same guard prevents the possibility of gaining access to those wishes and critical discussion of what to do with them.

Take, for example, the case of the suffering sworn bachelor who seems to speak in two opposite voices. He regularly complains about his miserable loneliness, but at the same time he consistently sabotages any chance to establish a realistic relationship. One possible explanation of this behavior, according to Freud's thesis, is that it is a distorted solution to the Oedipus complex. In other words, the inability to give up yearning for the fulfillment of the old sexual desire for a parent is leading the sworn bachelor to destroy each new relationship.

Transference-love is a therapeutic means to rediscover subversive wishes. In other words, the patient's merging of her analyst and her parent (or any other object of the infantile sexual desire) enables the emergence of the unrealistic hidden wishes to a conscious level. This new awareness opens the possibility for a new discussion about the old subversive sexual wishes. One reasonable option would be to give up those old sexual desires in the same way that at the end of the analysis the patient is able to be released from her love for the analyst.[17] In the context of our example, successful transference strategy miraculously opens for our sworn bachelor the option that was formerly blocked, the option of establishing a "normal" relationship.[18]

At this point, I must insist that transference-love, according to Freud, is a manipulative procedure, though such a claim does not necessarily imply a normative judgment because manipulative behavior is sometimes a necessary or desperate strategy that should be endorsed for its benevolent results. However, it is important to emphasize certain further important points. I begin by reiterating that Freud insists that cultivating love and affection on the part of the patient towards her analyst is a necessary condition for the success of the psychoanalysis. That is, the analyst is supposed to lead his patient into falling in love with him. Of course, the intention is not to fulfill this erotic love in the normal way (even though that sometimes happens), but to direct that love for the benefit of the therapy.[19] The crucial point here is that there is no escape from facing such an embarrassing "romantic" situation. In any case, and even without the analyst's intentions, the patient is going to direct her sexual and erotic attraction towards him.[20]

Beyond the controversy about this observation, it seems that the analyst can stop the falling-in-love process, or at least moderate it. (For example, he might clarify for the patient that he is not her father.)

Yet, Freud insists that this is exactly what the analyst should not do: "... I shall state it as a fundamental principle that the patient's need and longing should be allowed to persist in her, in order that they may serve as forces impelling her to do work and to make changes, and that we must beware of appeasing those forces by means of surrogates ... He must keep firm hold of the transference-love, but treat it as something unreal, as a situation which has to be gone through in the treatment and traced back to its unconscious origins and which must assist in bringing all that is most deeply hidden in the patient's erotic life into her consciousness and therefore under her control."[21]

The meaning of that passage is that the analyst is triggering and directing his patient's feelings in order to mislead her for her own benefit.[22] To be more specific, the erotic feelings that the patient feels towards her analyst enable him to strengthen the patient's dependency on the therapeutic bond and to create an opportunity to reach the sensitive depths in order to discover and dramatize the conflicted issues that the patient cannot, or is not, willing to discuss directly and critically.

The practical implications of the transference phenomenon, according to Freud, concretize, forcefully, the paradoxical aspect of expanding manipulation. The erotic feelings that usually distort and limit the critical thinking (especially according to Freud) serve here as means for helping the patient to confront her preferences and improve her decision-making. More specifically, exposing repressed wishes (such sexual desire for one of the parents) opens the possibility to give up on the unrealistic desire to fulfill them and pave the way for a change.

This particular strategy of opening choices leans on a hidden assumption that deep down, human beings, in principle, know what they want. The troubles come from the "unsupportive" environment restricting the possibilities to fulfill their desires, wishes, and wants. The Freudian innovation is that any mortal human being (especially and extremely the neurotic) does not, completely, give up on his or her "forbidden" sexual wishes, but suppresses them. From this moment the suppression will determine patterns of uncontrolled subversive behavior. Therefore, the purpose of the therapy is to expose the unrealistic wishes. In this way, the option to give up on the desire for their concrete fulfillment is opened. (For example, the sworn bachelor discovers his Oedipal wishes and, surprisingly, the prospect of considering a "normal" relationship becomes possible for him.)

The emphasis is that the therapist is not supposed to lead his patient toward a specific option, but only to expand her field of vision.

This move seems to be based on another implicit assumption that, after the Freudian treatment has resolved the self-destructive compulsions, the patient—or more precisely, the former patient—will be able to stop undermining her own interests. In other words, the possibility to examine her behavior critically and choose the best available option for her is now opened. It is by somewhat paternalistic means that Freud intends to return the individual's lost autonomy.

ANALYST VERSUS PATIENT: WHO IS THE TRUE MANIPULATOR?

It is hard to doubt that Freud constructed an elegant and attractive paradigm that seems to fulfill an old human desire for finding explanations and solutions to human problems. However, as Freud understood very well, human life is complex, mysterious, and enigmatic. Therefore, much as he might refuse to admit it, it remains unclear whether his views on human misery are true or only somewhat plausible. Indeed, the transference-love phenomenon, especially as described by Freud, remains controversial.

A different and even opposing analysis of the transference phenomenon may serve to delineate the scope of the controversy. This contrasting view is, actually, my own construction developed from Szasz's barbed critique of essential aspects of Freud's theory. Ironically, examining the therapist-patient relations from this very different perspective raises the following question: Is a well-trained Freudian therapist a professional manipulator, or is there more to the theory?

As already stated, Thomas Szasz is well known for his bold critique of the notion of mental illness. As strange as it might sound, however, it turns out that Szasz tends to agree with Freud on central issues concerning human misery. For example, he admits that human beings have internal conflicts, act subversively against their declarations, and often enough show a strong tendency toward childishness. The disagreements are about the classification ("the diagnosis") of such observations and its practical implications. Freud diagnosed those characteristics as pathological symptoms, whereas Szasz believes that they are simply signs of difficulty and distress. To put it differently, Freud speaks about uncontrolled patterns subject to unconscious principles, whereas Szasz puts most stress on concrete reasons and full awareness.[23] In order to illuminate this essential controversy, I recall our sworn bachelor who claims that he wishes to get married.

It is evident that our bachelor speaks in two contradictory voices. On the one hand, he declares his sincere wish to get married, whereas on the other hand he tends to run away from relationships that start progressing in this very direction. According to Freud's theory, an uncontrolled pathological behavior is therein manifested. Only "mental surgery" will be of use in helping to expose the hidden subversive Oedipal wishes. The irony is that this is exactly the observation or diagnosis that Szasz refuses to accept. Szasz forcefully argues that internal conflicts and contradictions do not make one "mentally ill."

According to Szasz, the Freudian confusion between metaphors (mental illness) and real medical terminology (physical illness) has led to the erroneous diagnosis that certain ways of life, such as lasting bachelorhood, are symptoms of mental sickness, or at least severe signs of mental distortion. Ironically, Szasz points out that many married couples are far from conducting full and satisfactory relationships. Moreover, often enough "bad" marriages seem to be more stable than "good" ones. Therefore, the Freudian view generates an impossible dilemma for mental doctors who are supposed to determine who is mentally sick and who is mentally healthy.[24]

No doubt every decision is bound up with relinquishing choices. Though committing oneself to marriage is not exceptional, it is a serious decision that has its own particular costs, such as giving up certain freedoms. Our bachelor, who has his own doubts, habits, and fears, avoids making a decision. In this respect, he acts like a baby that refuses to learn the meaning of responsibility for his own choices. Unfortunately, ambivalence is not without cost, and sometimes it is more costly than the price of making a decision. The irony of fate is that getting married is not an irreversible commitment, as the possibility of getting a divorce remains open.

Szasz sees "pathological behavior" as the result of giving up responsibility in order to achieve an ulterior goal. For example, the person who sees himself as weak behaves oddly in order to draw attention to himself and perhaps gain some sense of security ("he is not responsible for his actions").[25] Of course, this analysis is valid for the therapeutic session in general and the transference-love phenomenon in particular. The burden of responsibility is not an easy one. It demands effort and much courage. In this connection at least, responsibility seems to be a synonym for maturity. Unfortunately, there is a strong tendency to search for short cuts, to choose what seems to be the easy way. Instead of directly facing the heavy task of making decisions and being responsible for the consequences, it is very tempting for a patient to ascribe the responsibilities to someone else.

One of the most accessible figures for such a mission is the analyst. However, it is well known to the patient that the analyst, who works under certain ethical constraints, is not willing to take on such a burdensome task. Therefore, the patient uses trickery to fulfill this desire and begins to behave like a child in search of a protective father or a fairy godmother.[26] Following Szasz's way of thinking, it seems that the transference-love is simply the childish behavior of the patient who looks for a parent to release him from the burden of responsibility. The inevitable outcome is that the therapeutic interaction recapitulates the relationship between parent and child. In the Szaszian view, in contrast to the Freudian one, the patient is directing the analysis. To put it differently, according to Szasz, Freud, who was convinced that he was using a sophisticated manipulative tactic, was actually the victim of his patients' manipulative behavior.

FRAMING THE THERAPEUTIC INTERACTION

Szasz's critique of psychoanalysis, whether it is completely true or too much of an exaggeration, is extremely valuable. It forcefully illustrates that the analyst, no less than other human beings, is not a superman and makes mistakes in guiding his patient. Therefore, making the therapy more beneficial requires setting general restrictions and boundaries to the interaction. In other words, the limitations of any analyst require that the psychoanalysis be conducted under the constraints of general rules that demarcate the field of the therapeutic interaction. This is not new and much has been written about the boundaries of the psychoanalytic situation. However, I propose to attack this issue from an unusual perspective. I propose examining the possibility of synthesizing the opposite approaches of Freud and Szasz to the transference-love phenomenon for the benefit of the analysis.

The basic idea is that the patient-analyst relations are dynamic and complex. Therefore, reducing the transference-love phenomenon to one formula seems a mistake. In other words, there is certain amount of truth in the radical view of Freud and the extreme observation of Szasz; that is, both the therapist and the patient manipulate. Therefore, it might be more useful to combine the two radical approaches in order to formulate a better framework for the psychoanalysis. But is it possible and, if so, how?

Freud used discoveries in the laboratory conditions of the "psychoanalytic couch" to construct general theories about the essence of human interaction. However, it might be useful actually to reverse the process by borrowing ideas from a general social theory and apply them to the particular case of the psychoanalytic interface. In this regard, I bring insights from social contract theory to my attempt to synthesize the extreme approaches of Freud and Szasz to psychotherapy.

BETWEEN "SOCIAL CONTRACT THEORY" AND "PSYCHOLOGICAL THERAPY"

Liberals, particularly individualists, tend to regard society as a composite of individuals holding different outlooks and diverse priorities in living their lives.[27] Those views are not only different but they often lead to conflicts of interests. Accordingly, the question is how to formulate a set of rules that will help the different participants work together for the benefit of society. This essential problem can be labeled as the "social contract problem."[28]

In a similar mode, psychological treatment offers a meeting place for two individuals united in the purpose of improving the patient's quality of life.[29] However, it seems, at least according to Freud and Szasz, that the participants (the analyst and the patient) have different views and contradictory motivations as to how to achieve the same goal. Therefore, one of the major problems is finding an efficient way to navigate the different motivations for the benefit of the analysis. More specifically, the quest is to formulate an effective framework, a set of rules and ethical constraints, to produce a successful analysis.[30] Thus, it is reasonable to examine the "efficient psychoanalytic frame work" as a limited specific case of the social contract problem.

The main problem is in finding general rules to demarcate the field of the interaction in a way that will bring the most beneficial results to the participants. However, there is a strong tendency, especially when dealing with such general and complex problems, to slip into the more concrete and familiar; that is, to confuse the general framework with particular cases. A creative method to cope with such possible confusion is to enlarge the problem to unrealistic proportions.

One possible way to enlarge "the social contract problem" to imaginary dimensions is to regard society as an agglomeration of selfish criminals who are destined to live together. Their self interests lead them to understand the necessity of following certain social rules for their own survival. Accordingly, the enlarged problem is finding an efficient framework to maneuver the selfish and downright vicious ambitions of a population of gangsters to operate for the benefit of their society.[31]

In the same manner, I suggest formulating the "psychoanalytic framework problem" as a contest between two swindlers who have acquired their expertise from two different schools: one from a Freudian university for talented therapists and the other from a Szaszian academy for professional patients.

FREUDIAN ANALYST MEETS *SZASZIAN* PATIENT

The psychoanalytical session is a meeting between a patient and analyst under certain ethical restraints. In principle they both wish to achieve the same goal, to find the appropriate solution for the patient's distress, and to alleviate his misery. The clash is about the means to achieve this end. The patient, who is paying for the analysis, naturally seeks some magic solution to end his suffering, while the typical Freudian analyst, who has no such powers, assumes, with conviction, that the solution must lie hidden somewhere in the patient's life story.

Each is convinced that certain limitations prevent the other one from revealing the crucial secret. Therefore, they soon become engaged in a manipulative contest. The analyst tries to "seduce" his patient into revealing his hidden intimate secrets by cultivating a love fantasy and some sort of erotic attachment in order to lower the patient's guard. Meanwhile, the patient appeals to the analyst as a powerful protective father or as fairy godmother. By flattering the analyst's ego and touching on his narcissistic impulses, the patient hopes to "coax" his analyst into taking responsibility for the patient's decisions and behavior, thereby breaking the evil spell.

This description might sound like a parody of a very sincere and delicate situation: the psychological treatment. Nevertheless, it combines two radical approaches to a crucial and quite strange phenomenon in psychoanalysis, transference-love. The preceding scenario describes an imaginary meeting between a classical Freudian analyst and my construction, inspired by Thomas Szasz's critique of psychotherapy, of a typical Szaszian patient. This imaginary scenario might not be far from reality.

Achieving an effective change in human behavior is not an easy endeavor, and it is reasonable to assume that almost any kind of psychotherapy involves a certain type of a mutual manipulative game. In other words, almost every analyst is compelled, one way or another, to employ some Freudian tricks, and almost any patient is an irresponsible Szaszian patient, at least to some degree. The question is: How can we use this observation to improve psychotherapy?

MODELING THE PSYCHOANALYTIC INTERACTION

The twentieth century has taught us that no person has a monopoly on the truth. As the many disappointments in science indicate, searching for the truth is a quest that is difficult to fulfill. This somewhat trivial observation is manifest even in the most intimate corners of our lives, including psychoanalysis. Indeed, we have learned from Freud that any analyst should be extremely suspicious regarding the patient's understanding of her own life story, and we have learned from Szasz that an analyst can be as fooled by his own convictions as his patient. Their different views of transference-love, the motivating vehicle in Freudian psychoanalysis, help to illuminate these important insights.

Freud pointed out that transference-love, the emotional reactions of the patient to the analyst, results from confusing the analyst with a central childhood image. Accordingly, Freud saw in the transference-love phenomenon a precious opportunity to discover hidden details from the patient's early life story that determine her "problematic" behavior. By contrast, Szasz's criticism of psychoanalysis points out that transference-love is the patient's strategy to maneuver the analyst into assuming the role of a protective parent. The patient, according to Szasz, has a strong tendency to recapitulate childish behavioral patterns in order to inveigle the analyst into shouldering responsibility for her own behavior and decision making.

Freud and Szasz examine the psychoanalytic interaction from different, opposing vantage points. Therefore, the results are not surprising. Freud prescribed sophisticated maneuvers for the highly skilled analyst, whereas Szasz describes and emphasizes the maneuvers of the "professional" patient.[32] However, as stated throughout, every social phenomenon in human life cannot be fully explained by one formula. Accordingly, I have viewed the contradictory approaches of Freud and Szasz as complementary. For this purpose, I have sketched general guidelines for an imaginary scene: Freudian analyst meets Szaszian patient.

Our "exemplary meeting" between Freudian analyst and Szaszian patient is only a model. Like most models, it is a simplification of complicated and problematic interactions. However, models, like myths, may offer lessons, and the lesson from our imaginary-realistic scenario is that human beings, including well-trained analysts operating out of the best intentions, are limited and can easily make mistakes. To diminish harm, the psychoanalytic interaction should be conducted according to general rules that give a structure to the undertaking.

Our simple model, a competition between two swindlers (Freudian therapist and Szaszian patient) can improve the psychoanalysis framework. Analyzing the different moves of the two players in this imaginary interaction can be a valuable instrument for examining, evaluating, and improving the rules of the psychotherapeutic game. This research program is extremely important for a critical discussion upon three central motives in the controversy between Freud and Szasz: manipulation, responsibility, and successful therapy.

NOTES

1. For the most part, Freud writes about his female patients, at least in the articles I am referring to. Therefore, I employ the third-person singular feminine.

2. Of course, one of the lessons is that any manipulator might fall victim to his own trap. This lesson is valid to manipulative behaviors in the best of intentions and even for the most benevolent causes. Compare to Agassi, J., "Deception: A View from the Rationalist Perspective," in *The Mythomanias: The Nature of Deception and Self-deception*, Ed. Michael S. Myslobodsky (Hillsdale, NJ: Lawrence Erlbaum, 1996), 24: "Many philosophers have noted that people who habitually deceive might fall for their own deceptions."

3. Compare to Agassi's comments upon Bertrand Russel's "fool's paradise" ("Deception," 1996): "A fool's paradise is not a place, but a state of mind; it is a system of opinions, of assessments of situations, that calms one down, that reassures one into the opinion that all is well, even when all is far from well. Fools may be ignorant of the severity of their situations, perhaps because being well informed tends to get them into a panic. This happens regularly, and there is little that can be done about it, except that the wise would still prefer to be well informed so as to try to cope with the panic more constructively."

4. See Freud, Sigmund, "The Future of an Illusion," in *The Standard Edition of the Complete Psychological Works of Sigmund Freud* 21: 3–56, Translated by James Strachey (London: Hogarth Press, [1927] 1968).

5. Compare to Popper, K. R., *Conjectures and Refutations: The Growth of Scientific Knowledge* (New York and London: Routledge, [1963] 1989), 49: "I may perhaps mention here a point of agreement with psychoanalysis. Psychoanalysts assert that neurotics and others interpret the world in accordance with a personal set pattern which is not easily given up, and which can often be traced back to early childhood. A pattern or scheme which was adopted very early in life is maintained throughout, and every new experience in interpreted in terms of it; verifying it, as it were, and contributing to its rigidity ... I am inclined to suggest that most neuroses may be due to a partially arrested development of the critical attitude; to an arrested rather than a natural dogmatism; to resistance to demands for the modification and adjustment of certain schematic interpretations and responses. This resistance in its turn may perhaps be explained, in some cases, as due to an injury or shock, resulting in fear and in an increased need for assurance or certainty, analogous to the way in which an injury to a limb makes us afraid to move it, so that it becomes stiff."

6. Freud changed essential parts of his theories many times. One version of the previous description is known as Freud's trauma and catharsis theories. Agassi summarizes it in few concise sentences ("Deception," 34–35): Freud "... attempted to explain the way some private prejudices have a strong hold on the minds of their victims: He was impressed by the fact that neuroses constitute intellectual blind spots, especially when the neurotics who sustain them are intelligent. He explained this by his theory of the emotional trauma (trauma means wound) ... The cause of every neurosis, he suggested, is a trauma caused by some frightening, painful childhood event. Initially, the trauma leads to an attempt to cope with it by conjecturing a hypothesis. Being infantile, this hypothesis is not surprisingly of a low intellectual level. What is surprising is that the neurotic never gets over the initial hypothesis. This, Freud explained, is due to two facts. First, reliving the traumatic incident is painful. Second, one attempts to avoid that pain ... Therefore, the purpose of psychoanalytic treatment should be liberating neurotics from the prejudices that are at the base of their neurotic conduct, which incapacitates them. This, according to Freud, can be achieved only by helping them relive their initial traumatic experiences. Once this is achieved, patients experience strong relief and a sense of catharsis...."

7. See Szasz, T. S., *The Myth of Mental Illness* (New York: Harper & Row, 1974).

8. Ibid., 44.

9. Ibid., 32–47.

10. Ibid., 119.

11. See, for example, Wyatt, C. R., "Liberty and the Practice of Psychotherapy: An Interview with Thomas Szasz," 4 (2001), http://www.psychotherapy.net/interview/Thomas_Szasz.

12. See, for example, Szasz (*The Myth of Mental Illness*, 259): "... I believe that the aim of psychoanalytic therapy is, or should be, to maximize the

patient's choices in the conduct of his life ... our goal should be to enlarge his choices by enhancing his knowledge of himself, others, and the world around him, and his skills in dealing with persons and things ... we should try to enrich our world and try to help our patients to enrich their ... "

13. Compare to Wyatt ("Liberty and the Practice of Psychotherapy," 14): "The situation is similar to what happens in school, especially at the university level."

14. According to Freud's view, one of the main goals of psychoanalysis is to "turn neurotic misery into normal human unhappiness." Indeed, according to Freud's paradigm every human being is destined to suffer, but the mental patients' suffering is beyond the "normal" level of misery.

15. Indeed, Freud ("Observations on Transference-Love," in *Standard Edition* 12: 157–174, London: Hogarth Press, [1914] 1915, 160–161) warns the analyst against being led astray by the patient's affections for him: "He must recognize that the patient's falling in love is induced by the analytic situation and is not to be attributed to the charms of his own person; so that he has no grounds whatever for being proud of such a 'conquest,' as it would be called outside analysis. And it is always well to be reminded of this. For the patient, however, there are two alternatives: either she must relinquish psychoanalytic treatment or she must accept falling in love with her doctor as an inescapable fate."

16. Freud ("Fragment of an Analysis of a Case of Hysteria," in *The Standard Edition of the Complete Psychological Works of Sigmund Freud* Vol. 7: 7–122, London: Hogarth, [1901] 1905, 118), explains: "What are transferences? They are new editions or facsimiles of the impulses and fantasies which are aroused and made conscious during the process of analysis; but they have this peculiarity, which is characteristic for their species, that they replace some earlier person by the person of the physician." At this point I would like to offer a few comments. The first is that Freud ("Observations on Transference-Love," 168–169) claims that "being in love in ordinary life, outside analysis, is also more similar to abnormal than to normal mental phenomena. Nevertheless, transference-love is characterized by certain features which ensure it a special position. In the first place, it is provoked by the analytic situation; secondly, it is greatly intensified by the resistance, which dominates the situation; and thirdly, it is lacking to a high degree in regard to reality, is less sensible, less concerned about consequences and more blind in its valuation of the loved person than we are prepared to admit in the case of normal love." But, on the other hand, Freud emphasizes that "we should not forget, however, that these departures from the norm constitute precisely what is essential about being in love." The second is that sometimes it seems that Freud defends himself against possible allegations concerning questionable moral aspects of transference-love. He claims that transference-love is not particular to psychoanalysis but is likely to appear in almost every situation involving contact with neurotic people. (Of course, the question as to

who is neurotic and who is not, especially according to Freud, is a difficult one.) Therefore, the phenomenon pertains to mental problems of certain people and perhaps not to the therapeutic modality: "It is not the fact that the transference in psychoanalysis develops more intensely and immoderately than outside it. Institutions and homes for the treatment of nervous patients by methods other than analysis provide instances of transference in its most excessive and unworthy forms, extending even to complete subjection, which also show its erotic character unmistakably... This peculiarity of the transference is not, therefore, to be placed to the account of psychoanalysis but is to be ascribed to the neurosis itself." Freud, S., "The Dynamics of the Transference," in *Collected Papers* Vol. II (London: Hogarth Press, [1912] 1956), 314–315.

17. See, for example, Freud (Freud, "Observations on Transference-Love," 170).

18. See Freud, Sigmund, "Turnings in the Ways of Psychoanalytic Therapy," in *Collected Papers* Vol. II: 392–402 (London: Hogarth Press, [1919] 1956), 392: "... our hope is to achieve this by exploiting the patient's transference to the person of the physician, so as to induce him to adopt our conviction of the inexpediency of the repressive processes established in childhood and of the impossibility of conducting life on the pleasure-principle."

19. Indeed, Freud presents four options (Freud, "Observations on Transference-Love," 160): "If a woman patient has fallen in love with her doctor it seems to such a layman that only two outcomes are possible. One, which happens comparatively rarely, is that all circumstances allow of a permanent legal union between them; the other, which is more frequent, is that the doctor and the patient part and give up the work they have begun which was to have led to her recovery, as though it had been interrupted by some elemental phenomenon. There is, to be sure, a third conceivable outcome, which even seems compatible with a continuation of the treatment. This is that they should enter into a love-relationship which is illicit and which is not intended to last forever. But such a course is made impossible by conventional morality and professional standards." Of course, it is not so difficult to imagine that Freud would vote for the fourth option, which is to direct the erotic love of the patient for the benefit of the analysis.

20. To concretize this argument Freud describes the situation of a patient who is constantly falling in love with her analysts (Freud, "Observations on Transference-Love," 160): "After the patient has fallen in love with her doctor, they part; the treatment is given up. But soon the patient's condition necessitates her making a second attempt at analysis, with another doctor. The next thing that happens is that she feels she has fallen in love with this second doctor too; and if she breaks off with him and begins yet again, the same thing will happen with the third doctor, and so on. This phenomenon, which occurs without fail and which is, as we know, one of the foundations of psychoanalytic theory..."

21. See Freud, "Observations on Transference-Love," 165–166.

22. No doubt Freud was aware that such falling in love is problematic. Therefore, he recommended that patients not make major decisions during the period of psychoanalysis. For a further discussion, see Hinshelwood, R. D., *Therapy or Coercion: Does Psychoanalysis Differ from Brainwashing?* (London: Karnac, 1997), 98.

23. See Szasz, T. S. "Does Insanity 'Cause' Crime?" *Ideas on Liberty* 50 (2000): 31–32. Szasz opens this paper with a quotation that concisely reflects his opinion: "The madman is not the man who has lost his reason. The madman is the man who has lost everything except his reason—Gilbert K. Chesterton."

24. See Szasz (*The Myth of Mental Illness*, 228).

25. See, for example, Szasz, T. S., "Hayek and Psychiatry," *Liberty* 16 (2002): 19.

26. Compare to Szasz (*The Myth of Mental Illness*, 223): "The medical situation, like the family situation which it often imitates, is, of course, a traditionally rich source of lies. The patients, like children, lie to the doctor. And the physicians, like parents, lie to the patients. The former lie because they are weak and helpless and cannot get their way by direct demands; the latter lie because they want their wards to know what is "good" for them. Infantilism and paternalism are thus sources of and models for deception in the medical and psychiatric situations."

27. See, for example, Hayek, F A., *The Road to Serfdom* (Chicago: University of Chicago Press, 1944).

28. Constitutional economics, which places "in close neighborhood to the social contract tradition in moral philosophy," concentrates upon a similar problem: "It focuses, in particular, on the question of how people may realize mutual gains by their voluntarily joint commitment to rules (Buchanan 1991: 81ff). Or, in short, constitutional economics ... incurring into how people may realize mutual gains from joint commitment, i.e. from jointly accepting suitable constraints on their behavioral choices." See Vanberg, V., "Market and State: The Perspective of Constitutional Political Economy," *Journal of Institutional Economics* 1 (1) (2005): 28.

29. Szasz sees the "therapeutic" interaction as a contract between two free individuals, and this contract, as is true for almost every contract, is subject to certain ethical constraints. The acceptance test is that the patient is willing to come voluntarily to the sessions and even pay the analyst substantial money for seeing him. See, for example, Wyatt, "Liberty and the Practice of Psychotherapy."

30. In the language of constitutional economists, the quest is to inquire how the participant "may be able to play better games by adopting superior rules." (Vanberg, "Market and State," 27.)

31. Of course, "the social contract problem" has many versions and variants. One of its well-known versions is Immanuel Kant's formulation of

the problem of the republican state (Kant, I., "Perpetual Peace," in *Classics of Modern Political Theory*, Edited by Steven Cahn, New York and Oxford: Oxford University Press, (1795) 1997, 582): "Given a multitude of rational beings who, in a body, require general laws for their own preservation, but each of whom, as individual, is secretly exempt himself from this restraint: how are we to order their affairs and how to establish for them a constitution such that, although their private dispositions may be really antagonistic, they may yet so act as checks upon one another, that is, in their public relations the effect is the same as if they had no such evil sentiments. Such a problem must be capable of solution." However, so far as I know, Kant only formulated the problem without offering solutions.

32. See, for example, Szasz, T. S., *The Myth of Psychotherapy: Mental Healing as Religion, Rhetoric, and Repression* (New York: Syracuse University Press, 1988).

CHAPTER 11
Liberation by Manipulation

"Expanding manipulations" aim at expanding the target's perception of available options. They are constructed to expand the target's field of vision without direct interference in his final decision. The manipulator is expected to accept and respect any final choice the target makes. I have distinguished between two means to achieve the expansion effect: emotional and intellectual. Emotional manipulations are designed to provoke strong feelings and desires in order to liberate a fixated target. Intellectual manipulations are geared toward convincing the target to examine reality from different perspectives. In intellectual manipulations, arguments and considerations are designed to maneuver the target to discover new horizons.

This chapter presents, analyzes, and evaluates an intellectual manipulative strategy. The liberal manipulator, who intends to help the target to discover new dimensions, constructs and presents a manipulative hypothesis. The manipulative hypothesis seems to be competitive, at least in some respect, to the target's initial position.

The manipulative hypothesis tactic, as I may dub such strategy, can be very effective in cases where the target seems to be possessed by a closed conviction. The manipulator believes that the target is trapped in a narrow perception of reality, which he is unwilling to examine critically, let alone consider other alternatives. Therefore, it might sound strange and even useless to try to convince him by presenting a competitive alternative while it is clear that he is not willing to listen. However, presenting a competitive alternative in a sophisticated manner might open for the target the possibility to change his attitude.

The "manipulative hypothesis tactic" is built to avoid any direct confrontation with the target about his attitude. The manipulator's intention is to bypass the defenses that the target is "well-trained" in using for blocking any possibility for critical discussion. The manipulator intends to penetrate doubts in the target's mind about the practical value of the target's viewpoint, without confrontation and criticism. To succeed in such difficult mission, the "manipulative hypothesis," first of all, has to distract the target's mind from his original outlook. It has to attract his attention and provoke his curiosity. Therefore, the presentation of the hypothesis should contain elements, which often appear in competent works of art: surprise, mystery, tension, drama. These elements intend to prepare the ground for the presentation of a manipulative idea in the maximum persuasive power.

An effective technique to achieve such an effect is suggesting to the target an absurd hypothesis that exceedingly contradicts his outlook. The manipulator indeed suggests an alternative, but the alternative is not practicable for the target. In this way the manipulator makes certain that he does not maneuver the target toward one specific practical option (as in limiting manipulation) but focuses only on expanding horizons. The power of what seems to be an absurd hypothesis can be realized in two dimensions. On the one hand, an absurd idea does not appear seriously threatening. Therefore, the engrossed target might feel safe enough to listen and think about the "strange" ideas. However, whenever the smallest doubt comes to the target's mind that there might be truth in such an absurd hypothesis, it can shake even what seems to be a solid position.

To illustrate the power of such manipulative technique, I present a masterpiece in the art of manipulation. This fascinating example is enshrined as canonical. However, many "experts" will never accept the idea that this case reflects an intentional manipulative strategy. I do not have any intention of entering into a debate on the intentions of the principal figure. I have no interest in judging whether he intended to manipulate or he believed that his astonishing hypothesis is the naked truth. His thoughts are his own private heritage, and we do not have the ability to objectively test his intentions. Moreover, as I have argued in the beginning of the book, almost every motivating action that intends to influence and convince necessarily contains manipulative elements.

My intention is to demonstrate a manipulative strategy that might be useful in cases of rigidity and inflexibility. It seems to me that familiar and sensational cases can be readily illustrative and persuasive. As I feel obligated, I reiterate with emphasis that any labeling of manipulative intentions here does not express moral judgment. As stated in the very beginning of this book, manipulations range from the most reprehensible vice to sheer altruism.

The example presented here analyzes a well-known interpretation of a short dream. This dream and its interpretation were taken from the highlight of Sigmund Freud's great work, *The Interpretation of Dreams*. However, it is this short case study that clearly reflects severe doubts on Freud's revolutionary approach to dreams: Did Freud, the master of interpretation, really interpret dreams or did he develop a manipulative technique to work with dreams for therapeutic application?[1]

CASTING DOUBTS UPON AN ENTRENCHED POSITION

It is quite common for a person to reach out for psychotherapy because of distress. However, many times, there are good reasons to believe that there is an enormous gap between the patient's hypothesis about her misery and the actual root causes of her misery. Unfortunately, in the more severe cases, the patient conceals a greatest secret connected to her suffering that she is persistently unwilling or, according to Freud, unable to reveal and discuss. Therefore, helping the patient improve her quality of life requires an indirect approach for exposing the secret.

In the previous chapter I explained that a powerful incentive (such as affection for the therapist) might stimulate the patient to talk and reveal her unpleasant secrets. I had explained in detail that a classical Freudian therapist will try to use love and the sexual affections of the patient (transference-love) to expose essential and sensational details from her biography. However, many times those important details, which have direct projection upon the patient's distress, remain a mystery. The true biographical source of the misery is not always clear, maybe never completely clear, and sometimes it seems impossible even to come close to it. As an alternative for revealing the truth, the authentic source of the misery, the therapeutic interaction focuses on raising doubts in the patient's mind about her view of central elements in her life. The purpose is to enable her to consider different options in general and the possibility for a change in particular.

This approach leans on the presumption that at the end of the process the patient will be able choose the best available option (according to her preferences) from the range of possibilities at long last appearing before her. Careful study of Freud's interpretations of dreams is consistent with this way of thinking.

INTERPRETATION OF DREAMS: MANIPULATION OR HIDDEN REALITY

Fraud's interpretation of dreams does not stand in a vacuum. It is strongly relates to his research, theory, and therapy. The impression is that Freud's main purpose extends beyond amusing himself with solving riddles and puzzles, much as often he might so indulge, but to use dreams for therapeutic application.

A therapeutic implement means nudging an entrenched and stubborn patient in any direction that will make her more flexible to consider a change in her attitude for her life. For this purpose, Freud uses sophisticated hermeneutic tools in order to structure a convincing story. It appears that his interpretations are covertly replete with all the convincing plot elements of a best-seller: tension, drama, intimacy, sex, jealousy, and, of course, a surprising and shocking twist at the end.

It is instructive to follow the way Freud turns the dream's story, which often seems meaningless and sometimes even complete nonsense, into a brilliant interpretation that will not shame even the best writers. However, the chord, which connects the different fragments and turns them into a brilliant and well-constructed interpretation, does not exist in the dream's story. The glue that joins different pieces from the dream's story and turns them into a well-constructed plot is taken from the dreamer's associations. Therefore, we might wonder again: Did Freud objectively interpreted dreams without ulterior purpose? Or did he construct manipulative hypotheses for therapeutic needs? In any case, whether Freud consciously intended to manipulate or his hypotheses are completely sincere, his work with dreams offers a fascinating study in the construction of expanding manipulations.

LIBERATION OR OPERATION

The following example briefly demonstrates Freud's method of interpreting dreams. His interpretation, which clearly contains absurd

Liberation by Manipulation 145

elements, contradicts the dreamer's perception of an essential part in her personal life. Freud is very cautious about instructing the dreamer in how to deal with his sensational findings. He is mainly satisfied with shocking her by exposing her latent wishes and regrets. Therefore, the interaction, which cast doubts on her view of central elements in her personal life, is colored liberally. However, Freud's observation is not a subject to negotiation. His views on the dreamer's wishes and desires are definite, and it does not matter if she likes it or not.[2] Accordingly, whether Freud's move reflects his "real" observation or it is the outcome of an intentional manipulative strategy, the interaction leaves deep paternalistic impression.

Let me go ahead to present the dream:

"Very well then. A lady who, though she was still young, had been married for many years had the following dream: *She was at the theatre with her husband. One side of the stalls was completely empty. Her husband told her that Elist L. and her fiancé had wanted to go too, but had only been able to get bad seats—three for 1 florin 50 kreuzers—and of course they could not take those. She thought it would not really have done any harm if they had.*"[3]

Freud's interpretations combine elements from three main resources: the dream's story, the dreamer's associations during the session, and the dreamer's biography. It is fascinating to follow the way Freud weaves and intertwines an elegant interpretation from those three sources of information. Here, I bring only sensational parts from the interpretation and the interaction.

We learn from Freud that one of the most important details is that the dreamer's husband "had in fact told her that Elise L., who was approximately her contemporary, had just become engaged."[4] Freud assumes that this piece of information, which is not appearing in the dream's story, is, actually, the trigger of the dream. In his analysis, Freud stretches this fine plot point in two different directions and suggests two contradictory hypotheses respectively: "the conscious hypothesis" and "the unconscious hypothesis."

"The conscious hypothesis" points that the dreamer has felt advantage toward her friend (at least in the past) since she has been married. "The unconscious hypothesis" expresses discontents from the haste with which she, the dreamer, had rushed into marriage.[5]

I present the two opposed hypotheses, one against each other, in Table 1:

Table 1

The conscious hypothesis	The unconscious hypothesis
The dreamer had been proud of her early marriage "at one time and regarded herself as at an advantage over her friend. Simple-minded girls, after becoming engaged, are reputed often to express their joy that they will soon be able to go to the theatre, to all the plays which have hitherto been prohibited, and will be allowed to see everything. The pleasure in looking, or curiosity, which is revealed in this was no doubt originally a sexual desire to look [scopophilia], directed towards sexual happenings and especially on to the girls' parents, and hence it became a powerful motive for urging them to an early marriage. In this way a visit to the theatre became an obvious substitute, by way of allusion, for being married."[6]	"Really it was *absurd* of me to be in such a hurry to get married! I can see from Elise's example that I could have got a husband later too." (Being in too great a hurry was represented by her own behavior in buying the tickets and by her sister-in-law's in buying the jewelry. Going to the play appeared as a symbolic substitute for getting married.) Moreover, beyond "the anger at having been in such a hurry to get married," the upshot is in "putting a low value on her husband and the idea that she might have got a better one if only she had waited."[7]

It is astonishing to observe how Freud is turning the dream's story on its head. For example, the dreamer's friend, who seems to be the heroine of the dream's story, is discovered as a marginal figure in the interpretation. Moreover, it turned out that the dreamer's friend is only a vehicle for the main issue: the dreamer's attitude towards her marriage in general and her husband in particular.

Freud marvelously uses a simple, innocent, and perhaps meaningless story of a dream to construct an entire theory. Freud's theory is discovering to the dreamer (or maybe the patient) a dominant motif in her life that she was not aware of: her ambivalence towards her marriage (the unconscious hypothesis).

Freud concludes that the foundation of the dream is a wish of having postponed her marriage. Of course, this wish is not realistic at least in our world. It is impossible to turn back the clock and reverse past decisions and actions. Therefore, the motivation of the dream, according to Freud, is an absurd wish. The inability to give up on an

Liberation by Manipulation

unrealistic wish, a wish that can never be fulfilled, is probably the reason that it is "buried" deep in the dreamer's unconscious.

Freud's interpretation is revealing to us, and more important to the dreamer, that she speaks simultaneously in two opposing voices: content and discontent from her married life. This sensational discovery "accidentally" fits well to a Freudian paradigm: unsolved ambivalence is one of the main sources of suffering.

Freud works in general, and his interpretations of dreams in particular, indicates that our unconscious is able to make extremely complex calculations. For example, the dreamer has creative abilities to compose a sophisticated riddle (the story of the dream) from a simple story of dissatisfaction (unhappy marriage). The inevitable questions that arise are: Do we indeed possess such creative capabilities which we are not aware of? Or is it Freud's creativity and sophistication that enable him to construct impressive fictions from banal, simple, and maybe unclear pieces of information?

Our complex hidden calculations, according to Freud, are not random. They are driven from unconscious guiding principles. For example, the latent story is, in principle, always contradicting the known and expressed hypothesis. The unconscious voice is always opposing the conscious one, and such a strong opposition is able to maneuver a person to act against his declarations and conscious aspirations.[8] However, we cannot avoid wondering if Freud actually discovered unconscious principles. Or did he construct sophisticated hypotheses according to therapeutic principles in order to help his patients to be released from their traps?

Freud's sophisticated maneuver has a dramatic impact. His surprising and unexpected interpretation raises doubts in the dreamer's view of her husband: "As regards the meaning of the dream and the dreamer's attitude to it, we might point out much that is similarly surprising. She agreed to the interpretation indeed, but she was astonished at it. She was not aware that she assigned such a low value to her husband."[9]

The willingness of the dreamer to accept such sensational hypothesis opens for her new possibilities. She can examine her marriage from different perspectives and thence consider practical moves, such as getting a divorce, finding a lover, or improving her relationship with her husband. However, there is a possibility that Freud, the charismatic therapist, actually ruined her marriage without any substantial reason for doing so, aside from wanting to make a sophisticated interpretation of a simple and innocent dream.[10]

MANIPULATION AND SKEPTICISM

The last example demonstrated that what appears as a meaningless dream can be spun and turned into a highly influential hypothesis. Freud used all his creativity to convince the dreamer that her dream enfolds a delicate and even intimate secret; her mixed satisfaction towards her marriage at a young age.

It is strange to imagine that a person is capable of not knowing consciously her true feelings about such a dominant issue in her life.[11] This is indeed a sensational discovery. It is not surprising that Freud's sophisticated maneuver has its impact and that the story ends with an astonished dreamer full of doubts about her husband and marriage.

However, if we want to be more accurate, the story does not tell how exactly the interaction between Freud and the dreamer ended. We do not have even the simplest clue whether Freud left the dreamer astonished, confused, and even frustrated, or how the interaction might have ended otherwise.

Freud brought this story "only" to demonstrate his technique to interpret dreams. However, it is not even clear whether Freud actually interpreted dreams or whether he developed a therapeutic technique to work with dreams. All the signs indicate that manipulative strategy is an entirely adequate explanation of Freud's unexpectedly brilliant interpretation.

A manipulative strategy for therapeutic purposes intends to cast doubts in the dreamer's mind on her perception of a central issue in her life. The important questions are: Is casting doubts in a person mind always beneficial? Is it always morally acceptable to steer a person into doubts about such a precious motif in her life?

BETWEEN ACTIVE AND PASSIVE SKEPTICISM

Entrenchment in a closed-minded and biased world view is not always surprising. Clearly, the fixated person finds some personal advantage in his strange position despite every costly disadvantage. His absurd position helps him to cope somehow with a problematic and even unbearable reality.

Ignacio Silone described the comfort that the miserable fascist finds in his unrealistic admiration to his leader: "If you attempt to criticize the Duce or discuss his character or behavior 'objectively' with a convinced Fascist you expose yourself to the same sort of difficulties as you would if you entered a church and said: 'Can't you see, my good woman, that the statue of St. Antony before which you are kneeling lacks even artistic value and is a worthless piece of *papier mâchè*?' The good woman would scratch your eyes out. Criticizing the leader in the presence of a true Fascist is equivalent to attacking his greatest pride, the source from which he draws comfort and consolation to alleviate the difficulties of daily life."[12]

As Silone described, appealing to common sense in such difficult cases seems quite useless. In order to achieve an effective change, a subtle approach is required. Manipulation geared to plant doubts in the target's mind on the value of his stubborn conception might succeed as an effective strategy. However, often enough, entrenchment in a closed and even erroneous world view obscures a painful truth. The possessed individual constructs a comforting delusion from pieces of harsh reality. In professional terms, the conviction serves as a defense mechanism.

Generally speaking, without defense mechanisms, even with their drawbacks, we would all exist in a perpetual nervous collapse. Might not dismantling and bypassing well-defended positions do more harm than good? Can raising doubts in the target's precious biased position worsen his situation?

Casting doubts, especially in a manipulative manner, is a controversial matter fraught with difficult obstacles. On the one hand, doubting the worthiness of a position that seems to be the last resort before collapse might lead to complete despair and paralysis. On the other hand, doubting the value of a problematic perception could serve as a springboard for a change and better coping with many of the difficulties. Is there an efficient method to distinguish between destructive skepticism, doubts that might lead to despair, frustration, and even paralysis, and constructive skepticism, doubts that might yield a beneficial change?[13]

These questions are not only particular to psychology. They have much relevancy to philosophers, social reformers, social scientist, educators, and every responsible human being. However, as important as this issue might sounds, we do not have any concrete method to distinguish, in advance, between constructive and destructive doubts. Therefore, reformulating the problem is required. I propose to replace the distinction between constructive and destructive doubts with the differentiation between active and passive skepticism.

"Passive skepticism" means to simply cast doubts in the target's mind on the value of his world perception. This strategy could be constrictive, narrowing options and even destroying a last resort to cope somehow with helpless complicity. In contrast, "active skepticism" is a two-stage process. In the first, doubts are used to shift an entrenched position. The second is to offer practical options and possibilities to cope with a difficult situation.[14] This strategy has better chances to help the target to discover practical alternatives in order to better cope with internal and external distresses. The difficulty is that any presentation of practical alternatives tends to diminish the effect of an irrational manipulative strategy.

The strategy to market new ideas often needs to be the more sophisticated than the ideas themselves. This is where manipulation enters the picture.

NOTES

1. I learned about the idea that Freud never interpreted dreams from the course "Where is the Freudian unconscious?" delivered by Professor Menachem Peri of Tel-Aviv University. Peri's central claim is that Freud never interpreted dreams but rather used the association of the dreamer to offer him a well-organized and constructed story.

2. Popper noted that Freud had presented paradigms that cannot be refuted. For a further discussion, see Chapter 7 note 13.

3. See Freud, Sigmund, *Introductory Lectures on Psychoanalysis*, Translated and edited by Strachey James (New York & London: W. W. Norton & Company, 1977), 122.

4. Ibid.

5. Freud selects the haste motif, which is a central issue in his interpretation, from the dreamer's free associations and two previous actual events: One week earlier, the dreamer bought tickets for the theater in advance. At show time, it turned out that one of the hall's wings was almost empty. Therefore, her haste, which cost her extra money, was superfluous. In the second event, her sister-in-law hastens to spend all the money she got from her husband as a present, on jewelry.

6. Freud, *Introductory Lectures on Psychoanalysis*, 220.

7. Ibid., 224–225.

8. See, for example, the example of the "sworn bachelor" in the previous chapter.

9. See Freud (*Introductory Lectures on Psychoanalysis*, 125).

10. Ironically, Freud (Ibid., 124) noted: "We have *only* discovered that the dream expresses the low value assigned by her to her own husband and her regret at having married so early." (The emphasis is mine.)

11. In a similar mode, it sounds strange to think that we can pose ourselves a riddle while we actually know the answer.

12. See Silone, I., *The School for Dictators* (New York and London: Harper & Brothers Publishers, 1938), 81.

13. I borrowed the distinction between constructive and destructive skepticism from Fisch, M., *Rational Rabbis: Science and Talmudic Culture* (Bloomington and Indianapolis: Indiana University Press, 1997), 17 and 20–21. Professor Fisch's discussion is dealing with criticism of the methodology of scientific research. Although the context is different, I find this illuminating distinction useful for my discussion.

14. Compare to Hayek's view upon the task of the political philosopher: "The task of the political philosopher is different from that of the expert servant who carries out the will of the majority. Though he must not arrogate to himself the position of a "leader" who determines what people ought to think, it is his duty to show possibilities and consequences of common action, to offer comprehensive aims of policy as a whole which the majority have not yet thought of it. It is only after such a comprehensive picture of the possible results of different policies has been presented that democracy can decide what it wants." Hayek, F. A., *The Constitution of Liberty* (Chicago: University of Chicago Press, 1960), 114.

CHAPTER 12

Conclusion

Manipulation is an elusive phenomenon present in almost every dimension of our social life. Manipulation appears in almost infinite variations and under many different guises. Manipulation ranges from immoral techniques of negotiation to acts of healing in psychotherapy and even medicine. Manipulation can serve as an effective weapon, as a future dictator's propaganda, and it can be the last resort of the disadvantaged in society to attract attention to his misery. Manipulation can limit the target's consideration and judgment while choosing his actions (limiting manipulations) and it can move a narrow-minded target to discover new horizons (expanding manipulations). In short, manipulation is a extensive phenomenon.

I have narrowed the discussion to manipulations that mentally interfere in the decision-making of a person. Thus, questions concerning the individual's independence and freedom of choice arise throughout the book. Is the target of manipulation acting by free choice, or is the manipulator guiding him by abusing his weaknesses? Is the target purely a victim of manipulation, or does he allow himself to be manipulated? Where exactly is the line between free choice and being controlled against one's inherent preferences, priorities, and desires?

We cannot measure a person's "mental independence," which creates the general problem of how to ensure the independence of any individual. How can we guarantee that an individual is acting freely and is able to improve his decision-making if he wants to?

As illustrated throughout, trying to cope directly with such questions would tax even the Wisdom of Solomon. Trying to solve problems that exceed human comprehension, especially in ethics and politics, can turn into a utopian mission that endangers our liberty, like in Orwell's *1984*. Therefore, some paradigm shift is required. Instead of concentrating on the problem of manipulation, let us take a step back to examine the bigger picture: how to build the foundations of a decent, stable society?

This broad and controversial matter diminishes the problem of manipulation because every suggestion to conduct a good society gives an indirect solution to the problem of manipulation. For example, capitalists will argue that the invisible hand, market forces in a free society, is the best available mechanism to protect our mental freedom. Constitutional economists will claim that a free society operating in a framework of an efficient constitution (general rules that are supposed to ensure a decent social game) can diminish the impact of damaging influences, such as indecent manipulations.

The debate over the decent social order is much more vital and critical than any the discussion on manipulation. Moreover, many liberal thinkers might argue that manipulative behavior is only a marginal problem as compared to all the other myriad difficulties that a free society confronts daily. However, whether manipulative behavior is a marginal problem or substantial, this phenomenon enables us to shed light into the dark corners of ethics and politics. Manipulation can serve as an instrument to explore major obstacles and difficulties that the open society must overcome.

This book is only a preliminary discussion on a pervading social phenomenon. This very basic discussion intends to prepare the ground for a much broader and important project: how to construct the foundations of a good society.

Bibliography

Adorno, T. W. (1951) "Freudian Theory and the Pattern of Fascist Propaganda" in *The Essential Frankfurt School Reader*. Ed. Andrew Arato and Eike Gebhardt. New York: Urizen, 1978, 118–37.
Agassi, J. (1985) *Technology: Philosophical and Social Aspects*. Dordrecht, Holland: D. Reidel Publishing Company.
———. (1990) "Brainwashing," *Methodology and Science* 23: 117–129.
———. (1996) "Deception: A View from the Rationalist Perspective" in *The Mythomanias: The Nature of Deception and Self-deception*. Ed. Michael S. Myslobodsky. Hillsdale, NJ: Lawrence Erlbaum, 1996: 23–50.
———. (2000) *Liberal Nationalism for Israel: Towards an Israeli National Identity*. Jerusalem and New York: Gefen (Translation from the Hebrew book of 1984).
Banks, Paul. "Store Wars," *Marketing Magazine* 14 (8) 2003.
Berlin, I. [1969] (1975) *Four Essays on Liberty*. Oxford: Oxford University Press.
Bickerton, I. J., and C. L. Klausner. (2007) *A Concise History of the Arab Israeli Conflict*. 5th ed. Englewood Cliffs NJ: Prentice Hall.
Buchanan, James M. (2001) *Choice, Contract and Constitutions*. Vol. 16 of *The Collected Works of James M. Buchanan*, Indianapolis: Liberty Fund.
BusinessWeek. August 7, 1989.
Caldwell, B. (1977) "Hayek and Socialism." *Journal of Economic Literature* 35 (December): 1856–1890.
Caldwell, B. (2004) *Hayek's Challenge: An Intellectual Biography of F. A. Hayek*. Chicago: University of Chicago Press.
Caspit, B., and I. Kafir. (1997) *Netanyahu: The Road to Power*. Galey Alpha Communications (in Hebrew).
Caspit, B., H. Kristal, and I Kafir. (1996) *The Suicide: A Party Abandons Government*. Tel-Aviv: Avivim Publishing (in Hebrew).

Dietz, M. G. (1986) "Trapping The Prince: Machiavelli and the Politics of Deception." *The American Political Science Review*, 80: 777–799.

Dworkin, G. (1997) *The Theory and Practice of Autonomy*. New York: Cambridge University Press.

Erickson, M., and E. Rossi. L. (1980) "The Confusion Technique in Hypnosis" in Rossi (Ed.). *The Collected Papers of Milton H. Erickson on Hypnosis: Vol. 1. The Nature of Hypnosis and Suggestion*. New York: Irvington.

Femia, J. (2004) "Machiavelli and Italian Fascism." *History of Political Thought* 25 (1): 1–15.

Fisch, M. (1997) *Rational Rabbis: Science and Talmudic Culture*. Bloomington and Indianapolis: Indiana University Press.

Fischel, D. R., and D. Ross. J. (1991) "Should the Law Prohibit 'Manipulation' in Financial Markets?" *Harvard Law Review* 105: 503–553.

Food Marketing Institute (2001) "Slotting Allowances in The Supermarket Industry" Report.

Freud, Sigmund. [1901] (1905) "Fragment of an Analysis of a Case of Hysteria" in *The Standard Edition of the Complete Psychological Works of Sigmund Freud* Vol.7: 7–122. London: Hogarth.

———. [1912] (1956) "The Dynamics of the Transference" in *Collected Papers* Vol. II: 312–322. London: Hogarth Press.

———. [1914] (1915) "Observations on Transference-Love" in *Standard Edition* 12: 157–174. London: Hogarth Press.

———. [1919] (1956) "Turnings in the Ways of Psychoanalytic Therapy" in *Collected Papers* Vol. II: 392–402. London: Hogarth Press.

———. [1927] (1968) "The Future of an Illusion" in *The Standard Edition of the Complete Psychological Works of Sigmund Freud* 21: 3–56, Translated by James Strachey. London: Hogarth Press.

———. [1959] (1908) "Creative Writers and Day-Dreaming" in *Standard Edition* Vol. IX: 141–153. London: Hogarth Press.

———. (1962) *Civilization and Its Discontents*. Newly translated and edited by James Strachey. New York: Norton.

———. (1977) *Introductory Lectures on Psychoanalysis*. Translated and edited by Strachey James. New York & London: W. W. Norton & Company.

Fried, Y., and J. Agassi. (1976) *Paranoia: A Study in Diagnosis*. Dordrecht: D. Reidel Publishing Company.

Friedman, R. & M. (1979) *Free to Choose: A Personal Statement*. New York and London: Harcourt Brace Jovanovich.

Fromm, E. (1994) *Escape from Freedom*. New York: H. Holt.

Gardner, H. (2006) *Changing Minds: The Art and Science of Changing Our Own and Other People's Minds*. Boston: Harvard Business School Press.

Goldhame, H., and E. A. Shils. (1939) "Types of Power and Status." *American Journal of Sociology* 45 (2): 171–182.

Goodin, R. E. (1980) *Manipulatory Politics*. New Haven and London: Yale University Press.
Griffin, J. (1986) *Well-Being: Its Meaning, Measurement and Moral Importance*. Oxford: Clarendon Press.
Grunbaum, A. (1985) *The Foundations of Psychoanalysis: A Philosophical Critique*. London: University of California Press.
Haberstroh, J. (1994) *Ice Cube Sex: The Truth About Subliminal Advertising*. Notre Dame, IN: Cross Cultural Publications.
Handelman, S. (2005) *The Ethical Limits of Manipulation from a Liberal Perspective*, unpublished dissertation. Tel-Aviv: Tel Aviv University (in Hebrew).
Handelman, S. (2006) "Between Machiavellian Leaders and the Arab-Israeli Conflict: Toward an Indirect Approach to Conflict Resolution in the Palestinian-Israeli Conflict." *Orient* 47 (4), 554–567.
Handelman, S. (2008) "Two Complementary Views of Peacemaking: The Palestinian-Israeli Case." *Middle East Policy* 15 (3): 57–66.
Hayek, F. A. (1944) *The Road to Serfdom*. Chicago: University of Chicago Press.
———. (1945) "The Use of Knowledge in Society." *American Economic Review* xxxv, No. 4: 519–530.
———. (1960) *The Constitution of Liberty*. Chicago: University of Chicago Press.
———. Interviews in *El Mercurio's Interviews*. Santiago: Chile, 1981. http://www.hayekcenter.org/takinghayekseriouslyarchive/005571.html.
———. [1973] (1993a) *Rules and Order*. Volume 1 of *Law, Legislation and Liberty*. London: Routledge and Kegan Paul.
———. [1979] (1993b) *The Political Order of a Free People*. Volume 3 of *Law, Legislation and Liberty*. London: Routledge and Kegan Paul.
Hedstrom, P., R. Swedberg, and L. Udehn. (1998) "Popper's Situational Analysis and Contemporary Sociology." *Philosophy of the Social Sciences* 28(3): 339–364.
Heilbroner, R. L. (1996) *The Worldly Philosophers: The Lives, Times and Ideas of The Great Economic Thinkers*. New York: Simon and Schuster.
Hinshelwood, R. D. (1997) *Therapy or Coercion: Does Psychoanalysis Differ from Brainwashing?* London: Karnac.
Hirst, D., and I. Beeson. (1981) *Sadat*. London: Farber and Farber.
Hobbes T. [1660] (1985) *Leviathan*. edited by R. Tuck. Cambridge: Cambridge University Press.
Holmes, R. (1976) *Legitimacy and the Politics of the Knowable*. London: Routledge.
Huntington, S. (1968) *Political Order in Changing Societies*. New. Haven: Yale University Press.
Kahneman, D., and A. Tversky. (1979) "Prospect Theory: An Analysis of Decision Under Risk." *Econometrica* 47: 263–291.

Kant, I. [1795] (1997) "Perpetual Peace." in *Classics of Modern Political Theory.* edited by Steven Cahn. New York and Oxford: Oxford University Press.

Kelman, H. C. (1965) "Manipulation of Human Behavior: An Ethical Dilemma for the Social Scientist." *Journal of Social Issues* 21, no. 2: 31–46.

———. (1985) "Overcoming the Psychological Barrier: An Analysis of the Egyptian-Israeli Peace Process." *Negotiation Journal* 1, (3): 213–234.

———. (1988) "The Palestinianization of the Arab-Israeli Conflict." *The Jerusalem Quarterly* 46: 3–15.

———. (2001) "Ethical Limits on the Use of Influence in Hierarchical Relationships" in *Social Influences on Ethical Behavior in Organizations.* Edited by J. M. Darley, D. Messick, and T. R. Tyler. Mahwah, NJ and London: Lawrence Erlbaum.

Keynes, J. M. (1980) *Activities 1940–46: Collected Writing volume 27.* D. Moggridge (ed.). London: Macmillan.

Klaidman, S., and T. L. Beauchamp. (1987) *The Virtuous Journalist.* New York: Oxford University Press.

Knight, Cf. F. H. (1953) "Conflict of Values: Freedom and Justice" in A. D. Ward (Ed.) *Goals of Economic Life.* New York: Harper and Brothers.

Koestler A. (1964) *The Act of Creation.* New York: Macmillan.

Kuhn, T. S. (1962) *The Structure of Scientific Revolutions.* Chicago: Chicago University Press.

Lasch, C. (1978) *The Culture of Narcissism: American Life in an Age of Diminishing Expectations.* New York: W. W. Norton & Company.

Leibowitz, Y. (1982) *Body and Mind: The Psycho-Physical Problem.* Tel-Aviv: Honiversita Hmeshuderet (in Hebrew).

Local authority election petition 98/94 'Jerusalem Now' faction headed by Arnon Yekutieli v. Shass Party (in Hebrew).

Machiavelli, N. (1979a) *The Discourses* in P. Bondanella and M. Musa (Eds.) *The Portable Machiavelli.* New-York: Penguin Books.

———. (1979b) *The Prince* in P. Bondanella and M. Musa (Eds.) *The Portable Machiavelli.* New-York: Penguin Books.

Mannet, P. (1996) *An Intellectual History of Liberalism.* R. Balinski (trans.), Princeton: Princeton University Press.

Mansfield, H. (1972) "Necessity in the Beginnings of Cities" in A. Parel (ed.) *The Political Calculus.* Toronto and Buffalo: University of Toronto Press.

Maoz, Z. (1990) "Framing the National Interest: The Manipulation of Foreign Policy Decisions in Group Settings." *World Politics* 43: 77–110.

Matzner, E., and I. C. Jarvie. (1998) "Introduction to The Special Issues on Situational Analysis." *Philosophy of The Social Sciences* vol. 28 (3): 333–338.

Neubach, K. (1996) *The Race: Elections 96.* Tel-Aviv: Yediot Achronot Press (in Hebrew).

Orwell, G. (2003) *Nineteen Eighty-Four: A Novel.* New York: Plume.

Phillips, M. J. (1997) *Ethics and Manipulation in Advertising: Answering a Flawed Indictment.* Westport, CT: Quorum.

Popper, K. R. [1945] (1996) *The Open Society and Its Enemies (vol. 2)*. London: Routledge.
———. [1963] (1989) *Conjectures and Refutations: The Growth of Scientific Knowledge*. New York and London: Routledge.
———. and J. C. Eccles. [1977] (1990) *The Self and Its Brain*. New York and London: Routledge.
———. (1994) "Models, Instruments and Truth," in M. A. Notturno (Ed.) *The Myth of the Framework: In defense of Science and Rationality*. London and New York: Routledge.
Raz, J. (1986) *The Morality of Freedom*. New York: Oxford University Press.
Riker, W. H. (1986) *The Art of Political Manipulation*. New Haven: Yale University Press.
Rousseau, J. J. (1762) *The Social Contract, or Principles of Political Right*, G. D. H. Cole (trans.), public domain. www.constitution.org/jjr/socon.htm
Rubinstein, A. (1998) *Modeling Bounded Rationality*. Cambridge: The MIT Press
Rudinow, J. (1978) "Manipulation." *Ethics* 88: 338–347.
Sadat, A. (1977) "Statement to the Knesset by President Sadat." Special Meeting of the Knesset: the Forty-Third Meeting of the Ninth Knesset (November 20, 1977), Jerusalem.
Schudson, M. (1986) *Advertising, The Uneasy Persuasion: Its Dubious Impact on American Society*. New York: Basic Books.
Shoham, G. S. (2002) *The Dialogue Between the Myth and the Chaos*. Tel-Aviv, Ramot: Tel Aviv University Press (in Hebrew).
Silone, I. (1938) *The School for Dictators*. New York and London: Harper & Brothers Publishers.
Skinner, Q. (1981) *Machiavelli*. Oxford: Oxford University Press.
Smith, A. [1776] (1976) *An Inquiry into the Nature and Causes of the Wealth of Nations*. Chicago: University of Chicago Press.
Storr, A. [1972] (1993) *The Dynamics of Creation*. New York: Ballantine Books, Random House.
Strauss, L. (1989) *An Introduction to Political Philosophy*. Detroit: Wayne State University Press.
Suber, P. (1999) "Paternalism" in C. B. Gray (Ed.) *Philosophy of Law: An Encyclopedia*. New York: Garland Publishing.
Sullum, J. "Curing the Therapeutic State: Thomas Szasz Interview." *Reason Magazine* (July 2000).
Szabadoa, B. (1985) "The Self, Its Passions and Self Deception" in M. Mike (Ed.) *Self-Deception, and Self-Understanding*. KS: University Press of Kansas.
Szasz, T. S. (1974) *The Myth of Mental Illness*. New York: Harper & Row.
———. (1988). *The Myth of Psychotherapy: Mental Healing as Religion, Rhetoric, and Repression*. New York: Syracuse University Press.

———. (1999) "Suicide as a Moral Issue."*The Freeman* 49: 41–42.
———. (2000) "Does Insanity "Cause" Crime?" *Ideas on Liberty* 50: 31–32.
———. (May 29, 2001) "Placebos, Healing and a Mother's Kiss" in Letters to the Editor, *New York Times.*
———. (2002). "Hayek and Psychiatry." *Liberty* 16: 19–20 & 24.
———. (2003). *Ceremonial Chemistry: The Ritual Persecution of Drugs, Addicts, and Pushers.* New York: Syracuse University Press.
Thaler, R. H., and C. R. Sunstein. (2003) "Libertarian Paternalism." *The American Economic Review* 93(2): 175–179.
Toffler, A. (1990) *Powershift : Knowledge, Wealth, and Violence at the Edge of the 21st Century.* New York: Bantam Books.
Trachtenberg, J. A. (1987) "Beyond the Hidden Persuaders." *Forbes* (March 23) Vol. 139 (6): 134–136.
Tversky, A., and D. Kahneman. (1981) "The Framing of Decisions and the Psychology of Choice." *Science* 211: 453–458.
Vanberg, V. (1988) " 'Ordnungstheorie' as Constitutional Economics—The German Conception of a 'Social Market Economy.' " *Ordo* (39): 17–31.
———. (2005) "Market and State: The Perspective of Constitutional Political Economy." *Journal of Institutional Economics* 1 (1): 23–49.
Walzer, M. (1985) *Exodus and Revolution.* New York: Basic Books.
Wantchekon, L. (2004) "The Paradox of 'Warlord' Democracy: A Theoretical Investigation." *American Political Science Review* Vol. 98 (1): 17–32.
Watzlawick, P., J. H. Weakland, and R. Fisch. (1974) *Change: Principles of Problem Formation and Problem Resolution.* New York and London: W. W. Norton & Company.
Weber, M. (1949) *The Methodology of the Social Sciences.* Illinois: The Free Press of Glencoe.
Whaley, B. (1974) *Codeword Barbarossa.* Cambridge: The MIT Press.
Wohlstetter, R. (1962) *Pearl Harbor: Warning and Decision.* Stanford, CA: Stanford University Press.
Wyatt, C. R. (2001) "Liberty and the Practice of Psychotherapy: an Interview with Thomas Szasz." http://www.psychotherapy.net/interview/Thomas_Szasz.

Index

Agassi, Joseph, 48, 78, 96, 116, 134, 135
Amulets for good luck, 91–94
Arab-Israeli conflict, x, 50, 102, 105, 107, 108
Artificial demands, 55
Autonomy, viii, x, xi, 3, 4, 14, 17, 38, 40, 45

Bacon, Francis, 112, 116
Beauchamp, Tom, 22–24, 26
Buchanan, James, 95
Burke, Edmund, 91

Capitalism, ix, 5, 154; and ethics, 39; and free market, 55, 56, 63
Coercion, vii, ix, 1, 14, 15, 17, 21–25, 27, 32, 38, 65; versus freedom, 57
Competition, ix, 39, 51, 53, 54, 55, 62, 63, 64, 69–74, 81
Constitution, 86, 154
Constitutional economics, 73, 74, 82, 86, 154; and rules, 95, 96; and social contract, 138
Conviction x, 111, 112, 132, 141, 149
Critical judgment and thinking, 6, 31, 32, 35, 127

Decent society, viii, 39, 53, 55, 64, 78, 82, 86, 99, 100, 102, 103, 154. *See also* Good society

Deception, vii, ix, 1, 2, 13, 17, 21–25, 27, 28, 45, 90
Decision making, viii, x, 6, 11, 15, 16, 17, 27, 31, 35, 38, 58, 62, 113, 127, 133, 153
Definition: open vs. closed, 18
Don Juan, 5
Doubts, x, 148–150. *See also* Skepticism

Economic Imperialism, 3, 18
Education, vii, 1, 5, 7, 11
Election, x, 16, 74, 87, 90–94
Emotional manipulations, 46, 47. *See also* expanding emotional manipulations; limiting emotional manipulations
Erickson Milton: confusion technique, 9–10
Ethics: monistic perception, 38, 42, 100, 101, 108
Evans-Pritchard, Edward, 68
Expanding emotional manipulations, x, 46, 90, 113, 114, 115, 127, 141, 144, 153; emotional, 47, 141; intellectual, 47, 141

Fantasy, 31, 32, 34, 115
Fascism, 56, 62, 78, 84, 85, 95, 98, 109, 148, 149

Free choice, 8, 17, 24, 33, 34, 38, 62; illusion of, 5–8, 17, 23, 33, 113; versus weakness, viii, 33 - 36, 39, 69, 83–85, 153
Freedom, 14, 17, 38. *See also* Liberty
Freedom of choice, x, 17, 23, 31, 32, 36, 67, 153
Freiburg school of law and economics, 81–82
Freud, Sigmund, 28, 33, 34, 60, 96, 118, 120–124, 128, 129, 131–135, 136, 143; and dreams, 143, 144–148; and transference-love, 125–127, 130, 136–138
Fried, Yehuda, 48, 78, 96, 116
Friedman, Milton, 55, 57, 59, 75
Fromm, Erich, 9, 51, 52, 54, 55, 61

Goodin, Robert, 1, 4, 5, 19
Good society, xi, 56, 63, 99, 154. *See also* Decent society
Governmental control and regulation, 55, 56, 58, 59, 61, 65, 73

Hayek, Friedrich, 38, 39, 56, 57 , 59, 62, 63, 78, 79, 80, 82; and classical liberalism, 56; and evolution, 80; and freedom, 38, 39, 57, 58, 61, 69, 75, 77; and knowledge, 64–68; and liberal dictator, 103, 105; and liberty, 76; and rules, 95; and the task of the political philosopher, 151
Hitler, Adolf, 104
Hobbes, Thomas, 103
Human sensibility sphere, 35
Huntington, Samuel, 103
Hussein, Saddam, 104
Hypnosis, 9, 10, 51, 52, 54

Intellectual manipulation, 46, 47
Invisible hand, 69, 72, 154
Israel, 86, 89–93, 97, 105, 106–108, 112

Jerusalem, 89, 90, 91, 93, 97, 98, 106
Jewish people, 47, 68, 89, 90, 93, 97
Jokes, 47, 54

Kant, Immanuel: social contract, 138–139
Kelman, Herbert, xi, 15
Keynes, John: on Hayek, 78
Klaidman, Stephen, 22, -2426
Koestler, Arthur, 54, 74–75
Kuhn, Thomas, 112

Liberal manipulator, 113–116, 141
Liberal paternalism, 114, 115, 117, 118
Liberalism, x, 4, 17, 32, 33, 34, 39, 45, 50, 52, 89, 114, 131, 154; classical, 56, 62, 85, 115; classical versus modern, 37–39
Libertarian paternalism, 117–118
Liberty, xi, 3, 17, 38, 45, 56, 103, 113, 153. *See also* Freedom
Limiting emotional manipulations, ix, 45, 50–51, 114, 115, 153; emotional, 47, 83, 11; intellectual, 47, 83, 90, 92, 111

Machiavelli, Niccolo, 26, 50, 99–109
Machiavellian shift, 101–102
Magic, 68
Manipulation and change, vii, xi, 7, 10, 37, 149; and critical capacity, 8–12, 14, 16, 17, 27, 52; definition, 1–3, 4, 5, 16; and desire, 12, 13, 17, 27, 125; and illusion, 5, 17, 28, 36; and misleading, 13, 14, 17, 24, 93; and rationality, ix, 2–4, 9, 16, 24–26, 27, 45, 46, 85, 86, 90, 92; and wish, 12, 13, 17, 27, 28, 32
Manipulative criticism, 84, 86, 94
Manipulative hypothesis, 141, 142
Mental freedom, 38, 57, 58, 61, 62, 154
Mental illness, 36, 37, 59–61, 122, 123, 128
Modern socialism, 56
Mussolini, Benito, 104

Nazism, 84
Negotiation, 35
Netanyahu, Benjamin, 89–92, 97, 98

Oedipus complex, 126, 127, 129
Open society, ix, 3, 15, 17, 45, 154

Index

Orwell, George, 40, 41, 154; and thought police, 58, 59

Palestinian-Israeli conflict, 87, 89–90
Paranoia, 87–89, 90, 96, 113
Pareto, Vilfredo, 91
Paternalism, 117; versus liberalism, 113, 114
Peres, Shimon, 89–91, 93, 97
Persuasion, ix, vii, 1, 2, 17, 21–27, 45
Piaget, Jean, 19
Placebo medication, 37
Point of no return, 35
Popper, Karl, 18, 77, 94, 135
Propaganda, vii, viii, 84, 85, 90–93, 98, 153
Psychiatric imperialism, 60, 123
Psychoanalysis, 114, 118, 120–122, 130–135
Psychotherapy, vii, x, xi, 5, 7, 9, 10, 99, 112, 116, 123, 130, 131, 143, 153
Public debate, viii, 90

Raz, Joseph, 38, 39, 76
Responsibility, 34–36; and liberty, 38, 39

Russell, Bertrand, 134

Sadat, Anwar, 50, 102, 105–108, 109, 110
Sales promotion, 10, 54, 70, 72
Self-deception, 37
Silone, Ignazio, 95, 98, 148
Skepticism, 148–150, 151
Smith, Adam, 64, 95, 110
Social contract, 131, 138, 139
Social justice, 14, 59, 101
Szasz, Thomas, 37, 76, 77, 79, 122, 130–134, 135, 136; and mental illness36, 59–61, 123, 124, 128, 129

Toffler, Alvin, 79–81
Totalitarianism, 56
Transference: love, 120, 124, 129; and Freud, 121, 122, 125–128, 136–137, 143; and Freud versus Szasz, 130, 132, 133
Trickery, vii, 2, 13, 14, 21, 24, 35, 46, 130
Tversky, Amos, 66

Weber, Max, 22

About the Author

Sapir Handelman is an Israeli associate at Harvard University and the Lentz Fellow in Peace and Conflict Resolution Research at the University of Missouri–St. Louis. He holds a B.Sc. in engineering, a M.A. in economics, and a Ph.D. in philosophy. His research focuses upon three main areas: political theory, applied ethics, and the study of destructive social conflicts and their resolution. He leads the "Mind of Peace Project," which offers simulations of a potential Palestinian-Israeli public-assembly, a Public Negotiating Congress. The simulations are conducted in different places around the world.